CHES
DOG FRIENDLY
PUB WALKS

DAVID DUNFORD

COUNTRYSIDE BOOKS
NEWBURY BERKSHIRE

First published 2020
© 2020 David Dunford

COUNTRYSIDE BOOKS
3 Catherine Road
Newbury, Berkshire

To view our complete range of books please visit us at
www.countrysidebooks.co.uk

ISBN 978 1 84674 393 1

All materials used in the manufacture of this book carry FSC certification

Produced by The Letterworks Ltd., Reading
Designed and Typeset by KT Designs, St Helens
Printed by Holywell Press, Oxford

Contents

INTRODUCTION

Within these pages you'll find 20 carefully chosen and diligently checked routes from right across this varied county that feature firstly a dog-friendly pub, where you won't be given dirty looks when you walk in, and secondly a route that avoids endless stiles or frequent brushes with boisterous bovines. On almost all the routes there is a stream, canal or pond for your dog to drink from, or even take a dip, and somewhere open and safe where your four-legged friend can be let off the lead to run off some of that doggy energy.

Along the way you'll explore country estates and parks, lonely estuarine marshes, pretty villages, river banks and canal towpaths. You'll discover remnants of the salt trade, lost harbours, geological curiosities, historic buildings and wildlife-rich heaths and woodlands. And all the while you and your dog will be getting some hearty exercise and fresh air.

All the routes in this book are on recognised rights of way or permissive paths, or within open-access land. Even though leads aren't mandatory, the law does require that dogs should be 'under close control' on rights of way, and it's probably better to err on the side of caution when in doubt. Although pains have been taken to avoid areas intensively used by sheep and cows – and routes where this proved impossible have been discarded – land-use does change over time and a livestock-free walk cannot be guaranteed (potential trouble-spots are highlighted in advance in the text, and alternative routes are suggested where available). You know your dog best, but unless they're extremely obedient and used to farm animals, it's always best to put them on the lead, keep them close at heel and get through the occupied field as quickly as possible.

For the most part, though, you can rest assured that the bulk of the distance covered here is along canal towpaths, through woods, heaths and parks, or along tracks and green lanes that are safely separated by hedges or fences from neighbouring pastures and paddocks.

I would like to thank the many publicans who have kindly given up their time to answer questions and allowed photography on their premises, and also the many dog-owners I approached who – without exception – showed an interest in this project and allowed me to photograph their animals for inclusion. I hope you and your canine companions derive as much enjoyment from following these routes as I have done researching and reconnoitring them. Any errors, omissions or changes on the ground please do let me know via the publisher.

Now, go and get the lead – it's time for walkies...

David Dunford

PUBLISHER'S NOTE

We hope that you and your dog obtain considerable enjoyment from this book; great care has been taken in its preparation. In order to assist in navigation to the start point of the walk, we have included the nearest postcode. However, a postcode cannot always deliver you to a precise starting point, especially in rural areas. Although at the time of publication all routes followed public rights of way or permitted paths, diversion orders can be made and permissions withdrawn.

We cannot, of course, be held responsible for such diversion orders or any inaccuracies in the text which result from these or any other changes to the routes, nor any damage which might result from walkers trespassing on private property. We are anxious, though, that all the details covering the walks are kept up to date, and would therefore welcome information from readers which would be relevant to future editions.

The simple sketch maps that accompany the walks in this book are based on notes made by the author whilst surveying the routes on the ground. They are designed to show you how to reach the start and to point out the main features of the overall circuit, and they contain a progression of numbers that relate to the paragraphs of the text.

However, for the benefit of a proper map, we do recommend that you purchase the relevant Ordnance Survey sheet covering your walk – details of the relevant sheet are with each walk.

ADVICE FOR DOG WALKERS

The Countryside Code lists six steps to ensure your walk in the countryside is as safe as possible. These are:

❶ Keep your dog on a lead, or in sight at all times, be aware of what it's doing and be confident it will return to you promptly on command.

❷ Ensure it does not stray off the path or area where you have a right of access.

❸ When using access rights over open countryside and common land you must keep your dog on a short lead between 1 March and 31 July, to help protect ground nesting birds, and all year round near farm animals.

❹ Keep your dog on a lead around farm animals, particularly sheep, lambs and horses. This is for your own safety and for the welfare of the animals. A farmer may shoot a dog which is attacking or chasing farm animals without being liable to compensate the dog's owner.

❺ However, if cattle or horses chase you and your dog, it is safer to let your dog off the lead – don't risk getting hurt by trying to protect it. Your dog will be much safer if you let it run away from a farm animal in these circumstances and so will you.

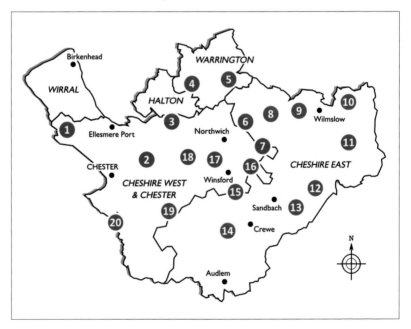

6 Everyone knows how unpleasant dog mess is and it can cause infections, so always clean up after your dog and get rid of the mess responsibly – 'bag it and bin it'. Make sure your dog is wormed regularly to protect it, other animals and people.

Please show a sensible attitude when encountering other walkers, dog owners, sheep, cows and cyclists.

Ticks and Lyme Disease

Ticks mainly feed off sheep, deer and pheasants until fully bloated and then drop off. They tend to cling to the edge of scrub plants, particularly bracken. Both dogs and humans are an attractive food source for ticks and you don't usually feel the bite. Ticks can carry Lyme Disease, which should always be treated by a doctor. However, you can help to avoid tick bites by taking the following advice:

Wear long trousers, tucked into socks, and long-sleeved shirts – even in hot weather.

Always check yourself and your dog at the end of a walk. The ticks are easy to brush off if they haven't attached themselves.

If a tick has attached itself, your main aims are to remove the tick promptly, to remove all parts of the tick's body and to prevent it releasing additional saliva or regurgitating its stomach contents into your bite wound.

To remove the tick, either use a tick removal tool (available from many vets and pet shops) or pointed tweezers. If using tweezers, grasp the tick as close to the skin as possible; without squeezing the tick's body, pull the tick out without twisting (it is difficult to twist tweezers without separating the tick's head from its body) – there may be considerable resistance. If no tools are available, rather than delay use a fine thread, something like cotton or dental floss. Tie a single loop of thread around the tick's mouthparts, as close to the skin as possible, then pull upwards and outwards without twisting.

1 LITTLE NESTON & THE WIRRAL WAY

4½ miles (7.2 km)

With convenient car parking and a wide belt of grassy marshland where dogs can run about to their heart's content, the Dee shoreline at Little Neston is rightly something of a magnet for local dog-owners.

This route is a little more ambitious and explores some of the other delights of the surrounding area: it sets off inland along dog-friendly paths between fields and includes a section of the Wirral Way, a converted rail trail, before returning to the Dee for a pleasant stroll back along the marshes' edge to the Harp. Keep your eye open for interesting birds: the marshes are home to several uncommon species, including Little Egrets, Short-eared Owls and Hen Harriers.

Start & Finish: The Harp Inn, 19 Quayside, Little Neston.
Sat Nav: CH64 0TB.
How to get there: Travelling towards Heswall on the A540 from Chester, turn left (signposted 'Ness 1¼') at a set of traffic lights. Follow the narrow lane to Ness village, where you turn right, past the Wheatsheaf pub. Continue for ½ mile to a roundabout, where you turn left (Marshlands Road). Pass under a railway bridge and continue until you reach the estuary. Bear left to the Harp Inn.
Parking: There are free car parking areas either side of the Harp Inn and a small car park for patrons.
OS Map: Explorer 266 Wirral & Chester/Caer. **Grid ref:** SJ289762.

THE PUB **THE HARP INN** is open all day from 12 noon but serves food until 3pm (apart from Curry Night on Tuesday evenings). The fairly short menu includes light bites, a children's menu and a range of sandwiches; mains are mostly pub staples. There are one or two vegetarian choices in each category. Dogs are welcome throughout, and water bowls and treats are provided.
☎ 01513 366980

THE WHEATSHEAF at Ness has a longer menu, though still focusing on 'pub classics', and serves food into the early evenings. There are numerous pubs and cafés just off the route in Neston and, a little further afield, at Parkgate. ⊕ wheatsheafpubandkitchen.co.uk
☎ 01513 366336

> **Terrain:** Rail trails, green lanes and estuarine paths with occasional streams, puddles and marshy pools.
> **Livestock:** Horses may be encountered on the Wirral Way and in the fields leading down to the estuary; there may be sheep or cattle in adjoining fields on the opening section, but you should always be separated from them by a hedge or fence.
> **Stiles and roads:** One low stone step-stile at Neston Old Quay should be easily negotiated by all but the least agile of dogs. The route includes a couple of short tarmac sections, but the vast majority is on paths and tracks, mostly firm and dry underfoot.
> **Nearest vets:** Neston Veterinary Surgery, 43–45 West Vale, Neston, Cheshire CH64 9SE. ☎ 0151 336 3335.

The Walk

1 From the front of the pub, facing the estuary, turn left and walk along the road, passing Denhall Quay and a car parking area on your right.

2 After a row of houses on your right, turn left, before a pair of bollards, onto a footpath, surfaced at first. Follow it along the edge of a housing estate, keeping to the right of the houses at every opportunity, until you join a farm track. Follow the track under a railway bridge and climb up to the road.

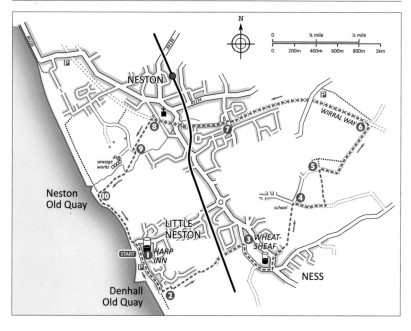

③ Turn right and follow the lane, passing junctions with Snab Lane and Well Close to reach the crossroads at the centre of Ness village. Turn left, past the Wheatsheaf pub, then right into Cumbers Lane. When the lane bends left, carry straight on past a row of terraced cottages to a kissing gate into fields. Bear left to a further kissing gate and continue past a play area to a road at the corner of the school grounds.

④ Turn right and take a hedged path leading straight ahead when the road bends left. After 350 metres, turn left into an attractive sunken path between gappy hedges and trees.

⑤ On meeting a major bridleway by a bench, turn right. At a junction with a footpath, keep left on the most obvious path. This leads gently downhill to the Wirral Way.

⑥ Just before the underbridge, turn left up steps onto the former railway embankment and turn left. Follow the Way for 600 metres, passing a carved log on the left and ignoring paths leading off to a car park on the right, before passing under a road bridge. Beyond the bridge, the Wirral Way follows a deep, gloomy cutting

with sheer sandstone walls passing under a high bridge, before climbing to a road.

7 Cross into Station Road, opposite, and cross the end of Bushell Road. Walk down to a bridge under the railway; if your dog needs a run-around off the lead, there is an alleyway into Stanney Fields Park on the right. Beyond the railway, bear left back onto the Wirral Way and cross an ornamental metal bridge.

8 Having passed over Church Lane, turn left at a waymark post pointing to 'Old Quay' (or for Neston church and town centre, turn right and left along Church Lane). Follow the right-hand side of the field down to a gap in the far corner, and then cross to a gate.

9 Turn left along the hedged path and follow it as it bends right into a field. There may be horses in the paddocks for the next few hundred metres. Follow the obvious surfaced path to a footbridge and through fields (with the water treatment works to your right) to the scant remains of the Old Quay above the saltmarshes of the Dee.

10 Turn left over a stone step-stile and follow the path beyond, which leads above the marshes to the road at Little Neston and back to the Harp Inn.

2 BARROW & BROOMHILL

3¾ miles (6 km)

Great Barrow stands on a hill between Milton Brook, Barrow Brook and the River Gowy, so despite its modest height above sea level the views are surprisingly good. A notable feature of the local landscape is a pair of community woodlands, both visited on this route, which are testament to the public spiritedness of the locals.

If time permits and your dog can be trusted around cattle and sheep, you could consider extending your walk to Plemstall (see map), a tiny hamlet with a fine church set among the remote Gowy watermeadows.

Start & Finish: The White Horse Inn, Main Street, Great Barrow.
Sat Nav: CH3 7HX.
How to get there: Turn off the A51 between Tarvin and Chester at the Stamford Bridge Inn, onto the B5132 signposted to Bridge Trafford and Barrow. After ¾ mile, you enter the village of Great Barrow, passing the right-turn to St Bartholomew's Church. Either park on the left, or turn right into Main Street, signposted 'Barrow', to reach the White Horse on the right after 100 metres.
Parking: The White Horse has a large car park for patrons, but there

is ample free, street parking nearby: try the B5132 towards the church from the junction with Ferma Lane and Main Street.

OS Map: Explorer 266 Wirral & Chester/Caer. **Grid ref:** SJ470684.

THE WHITE HORSE INN is a traditional coaching inn which also offers accommodation. Dogs are welcome throughout and water bowls are available. ⊕ whitehorsebarrow.co.uk ☎ 01829 741633

Terrain: Field and woodland paths, plus a winding green lane, with some road walking. There are short sections of streamside path at the start of the walk and at Broomhill, where your dog may be able to snatch a drink.

Livestock: Cattle and sheep may be encountered in some of the fields in the first half of the walk, but from Broomhill onwards you should be OK. Take care passing Hough Farm, a working dairy farm.

Stiles and roads: There are a couple of stiles, but all but the biggest dogs should be able to squeeze through gaps. Some road walking on fairly quiet, but vergeless, lanes.

Nearest vets: Manor Court Veterinary Centre, Church Street, Tarvin, Chester CH3 8EB ☎ 01829 740216. Barnhouse Veterinary Surgery, 1 Tarvin Road, Littleton, Chester CH3 7DD ☎ 01244 335550.

The Walk

. . . .

1 Turn right outside the White Horse along Main Street (heading away from the B5132). Between the village hall and the old pump, carry straight on into Mill Lane, a no-through road. *The brick cottages by Barrow Village Hall are a Grade-II-listed building, dated 1718. The White House, on the left a little way down Mill Lane, is also listed at Grade II, but is a century older.*

2 After 250 metres, turn left through a metal kissing gate at a footpath sign. The path, fenced at first, follows the stream into open fields, which may contain livestock. Follow the field edge to a further kissing gate, beyond which a fenced path leads out to the road.

3 Turn right, shortly passing a water treatment plant. At a road junction, turn left into Hollowmoor Heath and follow the road for 300 metres to a further junction, where you again turn left, passing Barrow Social Club on the left.

4 At a 'Disabled people' sign, turn right into NABS Wood, an area of community woodland. *Access to NABS Wood (named after the initials of the owner's grandchildren!) is provided on a permissive basis. Should this ever be withdrawn, a formal right of way offers an alternative along the bottom of the wood (see map). Ferma Wood, passed during the latter stages of the walk, also offers access on a similar basis, and is run by a local trust.* Keep left at a fork and follow a grassy path ahead to a bench, where you bear left to meet a public footpath running along the bottom of the wood. Turn left to a kissing gate into open fields, which again may contain livestock. Ignore a path to the left along the side of the wood, instead continuing along the bottom of the field to a kissing gate in the bottom corner. Continue along the bottom of the field to a stile. Cross the field ahead to a second stile. Follow the field edge towards a brick barn conversion, then go through a gate and follow a fenced path down to the stream. Turn left and follow the stream to a gap in the hedge. Continue along the stream ignoring a footbridge on the right.

5 On reaching the road by the bridge, turn left for 150 metres to a road junction. Turn right and follow Broomhill Lane for ½ mile.

6 Cross over and follow the farm drive of Meadow Lea Farm, descending between rocky banks past a house (ignore a footpath up steps on the left) to the farm. You may encounter cows here at milking time, so put your dog on a lead if in doubt.

7 Pass the farmhouse and turn left through a gate at the end of a barn, into a hedged track. Continue past a second gate and pass a stile on the left where a footpath joins. The path bends right to a gate, then left; unless you're diverting to Plemstall across the watermeadows, ignore a path on your right, and then another on the left.

8 The path bends left to Ferma Wood, and then right along the bottom of the woodland to a gate that gives permitted access to the community woodland. Continue along the main path, Ferma Lane, which develops into a track and climbs the hillside.

9 At the footpath junction, turn left and walk out to the B-road, ignoring a turning on the left. You can head straight on to return to the White Horse, but for a short diversion past the church, cross and turn right, taking the first left signposted to St. Bartholomew's Church. *The church is Grade II listed. A little medieval stonework remains in one aisle, but the church was largely rebuilt in 1671, with the tower added in 1744. The celebrated Chester architect John Douglas carried out two further restorations in the 19th century. A former 'standing cross' in the churchyard has been converted into a sundial.* Follow the track to the right of the church gates, bearing left past the lychgate and war memorial. At the end of the wall, turn left into a walled path, which emerges by the village hall. Turn left to return to the White Horse.

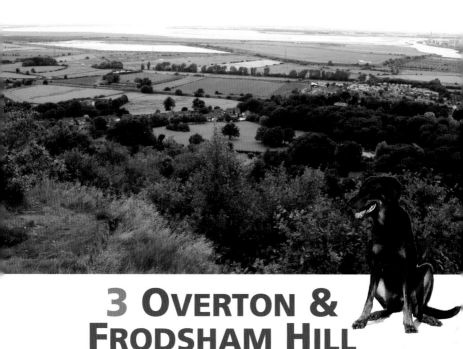

3 OVERTON & FRODSHAM HILL

2 miles (3.2 km)

The **Mid-Cheshire Ridge finishes abruptly** at its northern end in a line of sandstone outcrops, mostly obscured by trees, overlooking the Mersey estuary.

The woodland is well used by local dog-walkers and numerous routes are possible; this route starts low, along the 'Bottom Walk', before climbing to the top of the hill via Carriage Drive and the steps at Baker's Dozen. The path then contours along the top of the hill, with superb views over Frodsham Marsh and the Mersey to Liverpool.

The walk could be extended to include a visit to Castle Park (see map) if your dog still has excess energy at the end.

Start & Finish: The Ring o' Bells, 2 Bellemonte Road, Overton, Frodsham. **Sat Nav:** WA6 6BS.

How to get there: From Junction 12 of the M56 follow signs to Frodsham, turning right over the Weaver Navigation. Turn left onto the B5394 Fluin Lane (signposted to Tarporley) and turn left at the junction with Vicarage Lane (B5152). Take the first right, signposted to the Parish Church and Frodsham C of E Primary School. The Ring o' Bells is on the left by the church, after 200 metres.

Parking: The Ring o' Bells has a small car park for patrons, and shares a free car park with the adjacent church of St Laurence.

OS Map: Explorer 267 Northwich & Delamere Forest.

Grid ref: SJ520772.

CHESHIRE – Dog Friendly Pub Walks

THE PUB **THE RING O' BELLS** permits dogs throughout, as well as in the pretty beer garden to the rear. The pub opens for breakfast at 10am and serves food until 9pm. Four cask ales from the J. W. Lees brewery are on offer. Food includes light bites and a range of sandwiches, and there are at least two vegetarian options among the mains.
🌐 www.ringobells-frodsham.co.uk
☎ 01928 732068.

Terrain: Woodland paths, some steep and stepped or rocky. There are no major streams en route; take water unless the weather means standing puddles are likely.
Livestock: You are unlikely to meet any animals apart from squirrels and other dogs, though horse-riders are theoretically possible as some of the woodland routes are bridleways.
Stiles and roads: Short distances on quiet back streets; no stiles.
Nearest vets: Ashcroft Veterinary Surgery, 59 Main Street, Frodsham, Cheshire WA6 7DF. ☎ 01928 733228.

The Walk

❶ Cross Church Lane and take the tarmac path to the left of the church, running between the car park and the churchyard. At the end of the wall, turn left into Churchfields Park and follow the metalled path across the grass.

❷ Pass the play area and turn left beyond a park bench on a path that leads out to Howey Lane, where you turn right through a sandstone cutting (no pavement).

❸ After 100 metres, turn left into a rough driveway past a house called Beechlands. The drive bends right and narrows into a woodland walk (the 'Bottom Walk') until you reach a few houses on the left. Follow the driveway to reach a road.

4 Turn left past the entrance to a house called Dunsdale into a track that leads shortly to a gate, and follow the path beyond that climbs slowly through the trees.

5 Ignore a path down steps to the right at the end of the wall, continuing uphill to pass below a high red sandstone cliff on your left.

6 Keep left at a signpost (following 'Sandstone Trail Frodsham') and then turn left up a metal staircase (Baker's Dozen) that leads to the top of the

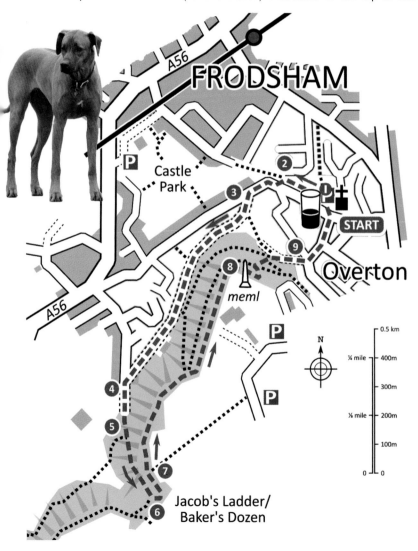

FRODSHAM

Castle Park

START

Overton

meml

A56

Jacob's Ladder/
Baker's Dozen

Jacob's Ladder scramble. *Baker's Dozen is named for Jack Baker, a former footpaths officer for Cheshire County Council who was instrumental in the creation of the Sandstone Trail.*

7 Keep left at a footpath junction (signposted 'Frodsham Centre'). Pass a bench and then keep right at a waymark post, along a fairly narrow path at the top of the wood alongside the golf course. The path winds along the top edge of the wood, stepped and fenced in places, and behind a hotel, before emerging at the war memorial. *The war memorial was erected in 1921 to honour the fallen of the First World War, and commands a spectacular, if somewhat industrialised, view ranging from the hills of Wales and Helsby Hill in the west, via the chimneys of Stanlow oil refinery and the fertiliser works at Ince, the wind turbines of Frodsham Marsh, the meeting point of the River Weaver and the Manchester Ship Canal, the industrial plants of Weston Point and Rocksavage, the prominent water tower above Runcorn, to the synchrotron tower at Daresbury Laboratory. In the distance beyond the Mersey Estuary the tower of Liverpool Anglican Cathedral is visible and, to the right, the top of the Silver Jubilee Bridge at Runcorn peeps over the intervening ridge topped by Halton Castle.*

8 Continue along the narrow path beyond the obelisk, to a fingerpost marked 'Frodsham Centre', where you turn sharp left. Descend to a flight of steps, at the foot of which you turn right and descend to a broad path (the 'Middle Walk'). Turn right to meet a road beneath a high stone wall.

9 Follow the road out to Bellemonte Road, where you turn left and walk downhill past the end of Hillside Road and the Bulls Head pub back to the Ring o' Bells.

4 PENKETH
4¼ miles (6.7 km)

What was once a scene of post-industrial dereliction is now a fine place for a stroll with the dog, despite the urban presence of nearby Warrington and the enormous cooling towers of the Fiddler's Ferry Power Station dominating the skyline downstream. Visitors today can simply appreciate the peace and quiet of the disused Sankey Canal and the grandeur of the mighty Mersey as it broadens towards its iconic estuary.

The Ferry Tavern is a dog-friendly haven at the end of a no-through road, squeezed between the river and canal. Markers within the bar show the alarming height of past floodwater, but in normal conditions the riverside garden is a placid place for both you and your dog to recover after a warm walk in the sunshine.

> **Start & Finish:** The Ferry Tavern, Station Rd, Warrington. **Sat Nav:** WA5 2UJ.
>
> **How to get there:** The Ferry Tavern is at the end of Station Road, a no-through road on the north shore of the River Mersey, south of the A562 road between Warrington and Widnes. From the west (Widnes), turn right into Tannery Lane, then right onto Station Road at the Three Elms care home. From the east (Warrington), turn left at

Penketh Methodist Church into Chapel Road (signposted "Penketh S'th CP School & Nursery") and follow it for ½ mile to Three Elms, where you turn left.

Parking: There is a free car park at the end of the approach road to the Ferry Tavern, a short walk from the pub itself.

OS Map: Explorer 276 Bolton Central, Wigan & Warrington or Explorer 275 Liverpool. **Grid ref:** SJ563866.

THE PUB

THE FERRY TAVERN is a dog-friendly haven squeezed between the river and canal. Dogs are welcome everywhere except in the carpeted areas, and water bowls are provided. A Husky Club meets regularly at the pub, which is a well-known destination for dog-walkers, who take advantage

of its large garden, with picnic tables and views over the Mersey. The pub is locally famed for its fish and chips.

🌐 www.theferrytavern.com
☎ 01925 791117.

THE BLACK HORSE, conveniently situated midway round the walk, also has a beer garden.
☎ 01925 635301.

Terrain: Level woodland, grassland and canalside walking on mostly crushed-stone or metalled surfaces. One short urban interlude along roadside pavements. There are occasional spots on the Sankey Canal where your dog can take a drink, but be aware that the sides of the canal are unstable in places and the banks drop vertically to the water. You are advised to keep your dog well away from the deep mud and unpredictable currents of the tidal Mersey.

Livestock: Other than an occasional horse, you are unlikely to encounter livestock en route.

Stiles and roads: The route includes a short section on public roads in Warrington, including the sometimes-busy Liverpool Road. For the rest of the time it mostly follows the Trans Pennine Trail and its offshoots, which are widely used by cyclists. The route crosses a railway three times via level crossings, a generally quiet freight line. No stiles.

Nearest vets: Maple Veterinary Surgery, Maple Crescent, Warrington WA5 2LQ. ☎ 01744 853520.

The Walk

● ●

❶ From the car park at the end of Station Road, go through the gates and cross the level crossing and then the disused Sankey Canal. The pub is to the right, but our walk turns left through a barrier onto the canalside path.

❷ After 300 metres, when the security fence on your right ends, turn right onto a path alongside a wood. Bear left along a track as you reach the riverbank then climb slightly (this is a former landfill site). Ignore a track joining from the left at the top of the slope, bearing right and descending gently to cross the outflow of the Whittle Brook.

❸ The obvious track returns to the Sankey Canal and follows it to the right. At a junction, after ¼ mile, keep right along the main track, leaving the canal to follow the Trans Pennine Trail and National Cycle Network (NCN) route 62. *The Trans Pennine Trail runs from Southport to Hull and is part of European Walking Route E8, which starts at Cork in Ireland and leads all the way to Istanbul in Turkey, a paw-pounding 2,900 miles!*

❹ Beyond a gate, the track passes a recycling centre and crosses the Sankey Brook via a footbridge to the right of the road. Cross and continue along the Trans Pennine Trail. The path leads through woodland and crosses another

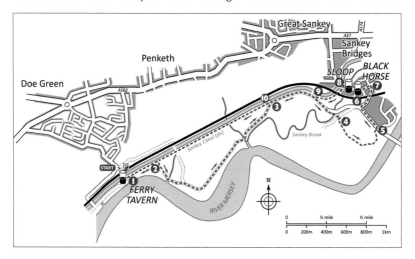

path. Bear left at the next fork, continuing on the Trans Pennine Trail as indicated by a waymark post. The path narrows – beware cyclists and perhaps put your dog on the leash if you haven't already.

5 When you reach a road beyond a 'Cyclists Dismount' sign, turn left (though you may wish to walk up to the bridge over the Mersey on your right for views of the river and the Warrington Transporter Bridge). Alternatively, a path on the left soon gives access to an open area where your dog can run around before you clip on the lead for the upcoming urban section. Returning to the main route, walk up Forrest Way past some industrial units on the right.

6 At a T-junction (Barnard Street), cross at the zebra crossing, turn right and follow the road over the railway to Liverpool Road.

7 Turn left and walk along the road, passing the Black Horse and then the Sloop Inn on your left. Take the next left, indicated by a Trans Pennine Trail sign, when you reach the bridge over the Sankey Canal.

8 Pass a disused swing bridge and, at the end of the short road, go through a gate and cross the railway at a level crossing.

9 Follow the canalside path for 300 metres until you join a metalled road (which you walked earlier). Continue alongside the canal for 400 metres or so, ignoring a footbridge on your right, until the main track bears left.

10 Here, take the path beyond a gate and barrier on the right, which continues alongside the disused canal. Follow the canalside path back to the Ferry Tavern, where you can reward yourself – and your dog, of course – with a welcome drink before returning to the car park. *You may decide to continue a little way past the Ferry Tavern to observe the boats moored around the boatyard and the decaying lock gates connecting the canal and river.*

5 THELWALL VIADUCTS

4 miles (6.4 km)

Unlike most British canals, the Manchester Ship Canal, which opened as late as 1894, was never built for horse-drawn narrowboats. Hence, there is no towpath. However, between Lymm and Thelwall a pleasant and useful permissive route has been established on the canal's southern bank, allowing access to this impressive waterway for you and your dog. The outward route follows the Trans Pennine Trail, here using the trackbed of the former Warrington and Altrincham Junction Railway (though the Bridgewater Canal – which does have a towpath – provides an alternative if you're concerned about watering your dog on a hot day).

Start & Finish: The Pickering Arms, 1 Bell Lane, Warrington. **Sat Nav:** WA4 2SU.

How to get there: From Junction 20 of the M6 follow the A50 towards Warrington, then turn right at the next roundabout (still on the A50). After 1½ miles, at the junction with the A56 by the Springbrook pub, turn right (signposted to Lymm). After ¾ mile, turn left into Bell Lane, signposted to Thelwall. Turn left at the war memorial to reach the Pickering Arms.

Parking: The Pickering Arms has a large car park for patrons, but you are requested to check with the bar staff before leaving your car.

OS Map: Explorer 276 Bolton Central, Wigan & Warrington.

Grid ref: SJ651875.

THE PUB THE PICKERING ARMS, open all day from noon, is housed in a half-timbered building of historical interest, and serves three real ales (currently Sharp's Doom Bar plus two guests) and a wide range of food. Dogs are welcome anywhere outside the restaurant – i.e. in the bars or in the partly covered garden – and water bowls and free doggy treats are provided.
⊕ pickeringarmsthelwall.co.uk ☎ 01925 861262

Terrain: Rail trails, tracks and permitted paths. One stile, easily bypassed. After a short early stretch along the Bridgewater Canal, watering opportunities are limited to ponds and puddles; the vertical-sided Ship Canal is strictly off limits.

Livestock: Occasional horses on the Trans Pennine Trail and other bridleways, and one field may contain sheep or cows, but the route is otherwise livestock-free.

Stiles and roads: The single stile is easily bypassed. There is one crossing of the A56 and two brief sections alongside it, plus further short lengths on much quieter roads.

Nearest vets: Lymm Veterinary Surgery, 10 Booths Hill Road, Lymm, Cheshire WA13 0DL. ☎ 01925 752721. Grappenhall Veterinary Surgery, 181 Knutsford Road, Grappenhall, Warrington WA4 2QL ☎ 01925 600000.

The Walk

. . . .

1 From the front of the pub, facing Ferry Lane, turn left along Thelwall New Road and then turn left into Gigg Lane. Beyond the former Sunday School

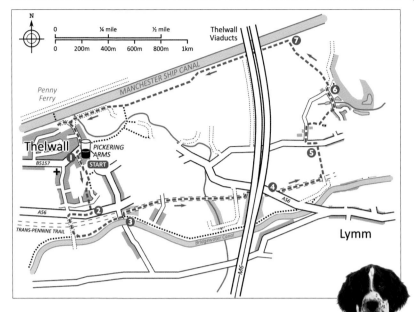

(dated 1835), take the footpath through the gap in the fence to the right of a driveway. Here there is an early opportunity to let your dog off the lead within this area of parkland. Bear left along an avenue of trees, then swing left to pass to the right of a football pitch. Follow the path right and left, and then left and right again as it twists through the houses out to Woodlands Drive. Pop your dog back on the lead (if you haven't already), cross the road and follow the path through the trees to the A56.

2 Turn right along the pavement and then cross the A56 into a track opposite the end of Stanton Road. Cross the Trans Pennine Trail bridge and continue to the Bridgewater Canal. Turn left through the small car park onto the canal towpath and follow it for 400 metres to the Thelwall Underbridge. *The Bridgewater Canal, opened in 1761, is often dubbed the oldest true canal in Britain (though the Sankey Canal – see Walk 4 – probably has a better claim to the title).*

3 Leave the towpath just beyond the aqueduct and transfer to the Trans Pennine Trail, where you turn right. *The Trans Pennine Trail runs from Southport to Hull and is part of European Walking Route E8, which runs from Cork to Istanbul.* Follow the trail for ½ mile to the M6, passing under two overbridges. As you approach the motorway, the Trail swings left to meet the A56 as it passes under the bridges, then drops away to the right before swinging left under the main road.

4 Continue along the trail for 400 metres to the first overbridge, where you turn left up the steps. Check for livestock in the field, then follow the footpath ahead, past a pond and along the field edge to the road.

5 Cross and turn left along the pavement, then take the first right (Pool Lane), passing the entrance to the Statham Lodge Hotel. After a couple of houses on the right, turn right along a slightly sunken, hedged footpath. After 100 metres, turn left at a waymark post and cross an overgrown field to a stile, and beyond it pass Oak Cottages (dated 1667) to rejoin Pool Lane opposite Brookside Avenue. Turn left, shortly passing a large fishing pond on the right.

6 When Pool Lane bends left, take the byway through the gate ahead of you. When the track divides either side of a field gate, take the left-hand fork, which leads between hedges down to the Ship Canal. *The Manchester Ship Canal opened in 1894, and still conveys occasional large ocean-going ships from the Mersey Estuary to the docks in Salford.*

7 Turn left along a permitted bridleway that leads under the twin Thelwall Viaducts. *The original Thelwall Viaduct (now carrying the northbound carriageway) was built in 1963 and was the longest motorway bridge in England at the time. The southbound bridge was added in 1995.* About 400 metres beyond the bridges, the path climbs slightly away from the canal, but continues parallel to it. Ignore a path leading off to the left after a similar distance, before meeting a metalled track with horse paddocks on the left. Follow this track out to a kissing gate into Ferry Lane. For an optional visit to the Penny Ferry (no need to cross), go through the gate on the right and follow the track round to the left. When you have finished, return to Ferry Lane and follow it past Thelwall Old Hall to the Pickering Arms.

6 PICKMERE
2½ miles (4.1 km)

Nowadays Pickmere is a peaceful oasis but for much of the 20th century it was a significant tourist attraction, with a permanent funfair and boat trips on the lake. A public footpath leads along the southern shore, and continues to Great Budworth, but a valuable permissive path along the northern shore allows for a complete circuit of the lake.

There's plenty of room to let your dog off the lead at the eastern end of the lake, but please respect other users and the local wildfowl, and keep them out of the water if there are any signs of blue/green algae, which can be extremely toxic to dogs.

> **Start & Finish:** The Red Lion, Park Lane, Pickmere. **Sat Nav:** WA16 0JX.
> **How to get there:** The Red Lion lies just off the B5391 at the eastern end of Pickmere village. From junction 19 of the M6, take the A556 exit (signposted to North Wales, Chester and Northwich) and turn immediately right onto the B5319 signposted to Pickmere, by the Windmill pub. The Red Lion is on your right after 2½ miles.
> **Parking:** The Red Lion has a car park for patrons, but there is also ample roadside parking opposite.
> **OS Map:** Explorer 267 Northwich & Delamere Forest.
> **Grid ref:** SJ693771.

THE PUB

THE RED LION offers a tempting list of main dishes, plus a selection of grills and burgers, and traditional roast lunches on Sundays. Dogs are welcome in the bar areas and in the garden. A range of hand-pulled cask ales are on sale, mostly from Robinsons Brewery and their various offshoots.

🌐 theredlionpickmere.co.uk
☎ 01565 733247

Terrain: Pavements and lakeside paths – mostly level.
Livestock: One or two of the lakeside fields may contain sheep at certain times of the year but the paths are well used by dog-walkers.
Stiles and roads: There are no stiles; the section to the lake from the pub is along pavements but none of the roads are overly busy.
Nearest vets: Northwich Vets, 469 Manchester Road, Lostock Gralam, Northwich, Cheshire CW9 7QB. ☎ 01606 359789.

The Walk

❶ From the car park of the pub, turn left and walk along Park Lane through Pickmere village, passing the entrances to several cul-de-sacs on the left.

❷ At Clover Drive, turn left then right into a small park which provides a shortcut to Mere Lane. Turn left past Beaver Close, then right into Jacobs Way.

❸ Go through the gates ahead of you and down the slope to reach an interpretation panel by the side of the mere. *Pickmere, unlike some of the newer meres which arose after injudicious salt extraction in the 19th and early 20th centuries, formed naturally and is centuries old.*

❹ Turn left along the lakeside footpath to a kissing gate into open fields. Pass a jetty and go through a couple more gates into woodland, ignoring a path off to the left. A boardwalk leads through reeds to a kissing gate into a field; ignore another footpath to the left here and continue along the lakeside past another jetty. Another kissing gate leads to a further field, as the lake begins to narrow.

❺ Just before the top end of the field, turn right onto a signposted permissive path over a footbridge. This path bears right through reedy scrub before running below a field to a wooden kissing gate. Continue in similar vein, with a fence on your left and the wooded lakeside to your

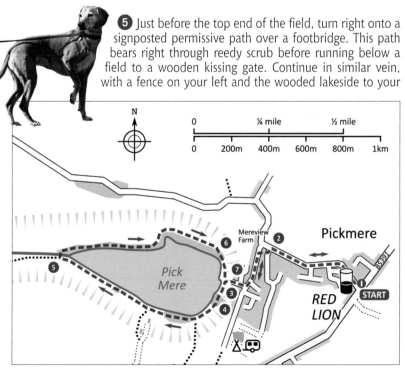

right. At one point the path bends away from the lake then turns back towards it.

6 Eventually, turn right through another wooden kissing gate into the trees and follow the path back to the waterside. Cross a grassy area to the interpretation board and turn left, back up the slope to Jacobs Way.

7 Now retrace your steps back to the Red Lion: turn left along Mere Lane then right again through the park to the junction of Clover Drive and Park Road, which you follow back to the pub.

7 SHAKERLEY MERE
1 mile (1.6 km)

Shakerley Mere is a former gravel pit, now flooded and surrounded by trees. It's a popular spot with dog-walkers, probably because it's simply so convenient – car parking is ample and free; the paths are level and not too muddy; there are dog bins, picnic tables, benches and disabled toilets; and horse-riders and cyclists are not permitted. The delightful Three Greyhounds, as befits its doggy name, works hard to attract the poochy pound, with dog treats and even dog beer on sale...and a warm welcome for humans too. This is the shortest and simplest walk in the book, so it's kid-friendly as well as dog-friendly.

Start & Finish: The Three Greyhounds Inn, Holmes Chapel Road, Allostock. **Sat Nav:** WA16 9JY.
How to get there: From Junction 18 of the M6, head west on the A54 (signposted to Middlewich). Turn right onto Centurion Way at the Salt Cellar roundabout on the outskirts of the town then take the next right onto the B5081, signposted to Knutsford. Pass through Byley after 2 miles and continue for a further mile to the

CHESHIRE – Dog Friendly Pub Walks

Three Greyhounds crossroads. Access from the west (Northwich and A556) is via the B5082, and from Knutsford to the north via the A50 and B5081.

Parking: Patrons can park at the Three Greyhounds; otherwise, park at the free Shakerley Mere car park on the B5082.

OS Map: Explorer 267 Northwich & Delamere Forest.

Grid ref: SJ729710.

THE PUB **THE THREE GREYHOUNDS INN** is open all day from 12 noon and serves good quality food from its seasonal menu until 9pm. Dogs are welcome in the bars to the left of the entrance, and in the garden and patio, and are treated as honoured guests: as well as water and gourmet dog treats, you can pamper your dog with a (chicken-flavoured) 'dog beer' and a bowl of sausages. A range of cask ales and ciders are on offer for the two-legged members of the party.
⊕ thethreegreyhoundsinn.co.uk ☎ 01565 723455.

The Walk

1 From the front of the pub turn left and cross the B5081 road, following the B5082 signposted to Holmes Chapel. About 50 metres beyond the junction,

Terrain: Mostly unsurfaced but firm and level lakeside paths.
Livestock: Ducks, geese and swans are numerous on the Mere – please don't allow your dog to chase them.
Stiles and roads: One stile (used twice) gives direct access to the lakeside path from the Three Greyhounds, but can be bypassed if necessary at the expense of a little road walking.
Nearest vets: Middlewich Veterinary Surgery, 39 Newton Heath, Middlewich, Cheshire CW10 9HL. ☎ 01606 833731.
Cheshire Pet Veterinary Practice, Manor Lane, Holmes Chapel, Cheshire CW4 8AB. ☎ 01477 544554.

a stile on the left gives access to a narrow path through the trees – note the point where the path emerges onto the main lakeside path for reference on your return, as it isn't obvious (if you wish to avoid the stile, continue along the road and reach the lake via the car park on the left). *Shakerley Mere is a flooded former sand pit now operated as a country park and nature reserve by Cheshire West and Chester Council. The lake is stocked with carp, bream, roach and perch and part of the shore is used by members of Lymm Angling Club.*

2 Turn right along the lakeshore and follow the obvious path to the car park.

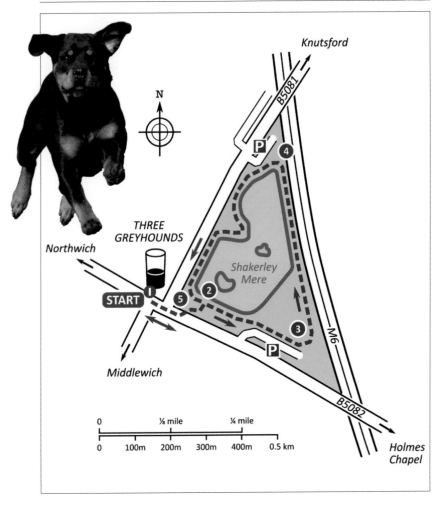

3 Beyond the car park the path leaves the lakeside briefly and bends left to run parallel to the M6.

4 At the top end of the lake, turn left (away from the motorway) and continue along the lakeshore, with another car park visible to the right. The path rounds a promontory and then continues to the southwestern corner of the lake.

5 For the quickest return, leave the lakeside path where you came in, to return via the narrow path and stile. If you miss it, carry on round the lake to the main car park, walk out to the B5082 road and turn right to return to the Three Greyhounds.

8 KNUTSFORD
3½ miles (5.6 km)

The parks around England's country mansions are often perfect for our four-legged friends: there are usually acres of grassland to romp in, ponds aplenty and woods full of scents to follow and sticks to chase. Tatton Park is no exception. However, do bear in mind that there are sometimes deer and sheep in parts of the park; keep your dog under close control, or on a lead if they are liable to give chase when there are animals around. Even if your dog can't be trusted around livestock, he or she can safely be let off the leash to run around freely on another of Knutsford's great open spaces, the Moor.

Note: The Park opens at 8am year-round and closes at 5pm (low season) or 7pm (high season).

> **Start & Finish:** Gaskell Memorial Tower (Belle Epoque), King Street.
> **Sat Nav:** WA16 6DT.
> **How to get there:** Gaskell Memorial Tower (designed by Richard Harding Watt) is in the centre of Knutsford, between the Cross Keys and Rose & Crown. From junction 6 of the M1, follow the A556 south, then turn left onto the A5033. Cross the motorway and continue to a roundabout by the White Bear in Knutsford, where you turn right. Just before a filter light, turn left by the brick-arched former town hall (now the Lost & Found bar) into Church Hill. On meeting the one-way King Street, turn left, then right into the car park.
> **Parking:** The pay-and-display car park off King Street.
> **OS Map:** Explorer 268 Wilmslow, Macclesfield & Congleton.
> **Grid ref:** SJ752785.

CHESHIRE – Dog Friendly Pub Walks

THE **THE CROSS KEYS HOTEL** and **THE ROSE &**
PUB **CROWN** are close together on King Street near the start, and both are dog-friendly. Dogs have the run of the Cross Keys, where several of the staff are dog-owners and treats may be on offer. On a fine day there are tables out front where you and your furry friend can watch the world going about its business.
⊕ crosskeysknutsford.co.uk ☎ 01565 750404

Although the Rose & Crown is more of a dining pub, dogs are welcome to loll at their owners' feet in the front bar, where canine portraits look down austerely on them from the walls, and there is a pleasant terrace in the garden at the rear.
⊕ knutsfordroseandcrown.co.uk ☎ 01565 652366

Terrain: Level parkland and woodland on mostly firm or metalled surfaces. In summer, toxic algae blooms may occur on the lake, and at such times it's especially important that dogs are kept out of the water.
Livestock: Dogs can safely be allowed to roam at will on the Moor, but there are deer and sheep within Tatton Park (though not always in the areas visited on this route) and dogs are requested to be kept under close control at all times, preferably on a lead. Please exercise particular care during the deer calving (June/July) and rutting (October/ November) seasons and obey any notices or restrictions on site.
Stiles and roads: King Street at the start and finish has narrow pavements and is busy with both pedestrians and traffic. Much of the walk is on surfaced paths, and there are no stiles.
Nearest vets: Knutsford Veterinary Surgery, Fryers Nurseries, Manchester Road, Knutsford WA16 0SX. ☎ 01565 337999.

The Walk

❶ From Gaskell Memorial Tower walk past the Rose & Crown and then turn right by Barclays Bank, signposted 'The Moors and Play Area'. *The Tower commemorates Elizabeth Gaskell, biographer of Charlotte Brontë, who lived with her aunt near Knutsford and modelled one of her best-known novels,* Cranford, *on the town.* Walk down the side of the car park and cross Moorside into the park where dogs can be let off the lead. Follow the tarmac path to the left of the park, with the lake on your left.

❷ At the end of the park, before a tunnel under the railway, turn left onto an unsignposted path.

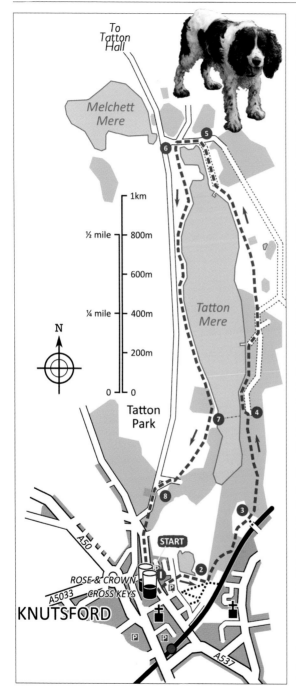

Follow the winding path through the trees and then a more open area until you meet another path that joins from the right by a railway overbridge. Bear left through a gate back into woods, obeying the instruction to put your dog on a lead.

3 Follow the wide path through the trees for a little under ½ mile to a second gate. From here you can either continue along the main track or divert left to the water's edge. If you choose the latter option, at the time of writing the lakeside path was closed beyond a jetty and you will need to return to the main track.

4 Either way, continue parallel to the lakeside before emerging into open parkland. If no sheep or deer are in sight, you can probably let your dog off the lead for a run here, but do obey any on-site instructions and don't let him or her harass the long-suffering ducks. Follow the waterside path past

an L-shaped jetty and a constriction at the neck of the lake until you meet a crossing estate road. (For a detour to Tatton Old Hall, continue ahead.)

5 Turn left and walk past the top of Tatton Mere to a road junction by Melchett Mere. For Tatton Hall and the Stableyard tearoom, turn right here. *Tatton Hall was first built in 1716 but was largely rebuilt a hundred years later, then extended in the Victorian era. It houses a noted art collection including paintings by Canaletto and Van Dyck. A fee is charged to view the interior of the house, or to enter the formal gardens. The original manor, Tatton Old Hall, begun in the early 1500s, still stands within the deer park.*

6 Turn left across the grass to a kissing gate by the lakeside and continue beyond, with the Mere on your immediate left and a park road away to your right. Follow the lakeside for nearly a mile.

7 Level with a fence across the lake, the path bears right to leave the water's edge, and skirts woodland to meet the metalled Knutsford Drive. It's a good idea to clip the lead back on here.

8 Turn left and walk through the grand park entrance, then follow the wide path to the left of the road which leads to the junction of King Street and Drury Lane. To view the Ruskin Rooms, another of Watt's creations, turn left, otherwise continue along King Street back to the starting point.

9 LINDOW
4¾ miles (7.8 km)

Pay attention if your dog drags a bone from among the heather of Lindow Moss: in 1983, peat-workers discovered a human skull on a conveyor belt here. Police initially suspected that the skull could belong to a local missing person, and her husband duly confessed to her murder ... before the skull was carbon-dated and found to be that of a male and almost 2000 years old! A thorough search by archaeologists located the rest of the body and the remains of Lindow Man are now on display in the British Museum.

This walk crosses three protected areas – Lindow Moss, Newgate Nature Reserve and Lindow Common – providing ample scope to let your dog off the lead, and passes two attractive lakes, Rossmere and Black Lake.

Start & Finish: The Plough & Flail, Paddock Hill Lane, Mobberley.
Sat Nav: WA16 7DB.
How to get there: The Plough & Flail is hidden away at the end of a no-through road, deep in the Cheshire countryside. To find it, take the B5085 from Wilmslow towards Knutsford (or vice versa). The country

inn is signposted from Lindow End, about 3 miles from Wilmslow and 4½ from Knutsford. Follow Paddock Hill for ¾ mile, then turn right at a triangular junction.

Parking: The pub has a large car park for patrons; as a courtesy, please check with the bar staff before setting off on your walk.

OS Map: Explorer 268 Wilmslow, Macclesfield & Congleton.

Grid ref: SJ817797.

THE PUB **THE PLOUGH & FLAIL** serves fresh, seasonal dishes using locally sourced ingredients, and a range of cask ales and wines are on offer. The pub is open from noon daily and food is served until 9pm. Dogs are very welcome; there is a 'dog watering hole' outside, and treats are available. The landlady, a dog-owner herself, runs a monthly dog walking club (booking required).

⊕ theploughandflail.com ☎ 01565 873537

Terrain: Mostly level peatland and heath, connected by quiet tracks and lanes. There are several streams and ditches, two lakes and other smaller ponds.

Livestock: Sheep may be encountered on a short section (noted in the directions) near Saltersley Hall, and you may meet horse-riders and cyclists.

Stiles and roads: There are a handful of stiles. The only tarmac is on quiet no-through roads and private driveways.

Nearest vets: The Vets Place, Chestnut House, Upcast Lane, Wilmslow, SK9 6EH. ☎ 01625 585500.

The Walk

① From the car park entrance, turn left down the lane past the front of the Plough & Flail. At the beginning of the drive to Barlow House Farm, turn left ('Private Drive'). Follow the drive round a right-hand bend to the gates of Lindow Manor Farm, where you take the byway to the left. Follow the byway round a right-hand corner and past some mobile homes on your right.

② After the mobile homes, look out for a waymark post, where you leave the byway to cross the field and drive on your left. Go through a kissing gate opposite, into birch woodland. Follow the path beyond, with former peat workings on either side.

③ Cross a footbridge onto a crossing track, take a couple of steps to the right and then cross a second footbridge to continue in the same direction as before. The path

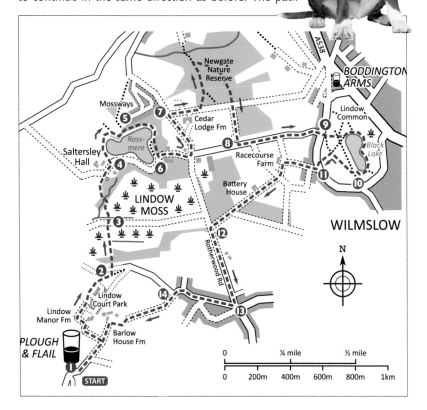

continues through woodland to a further footbridge, beyond which you bear right and leave the trees below Saltersley Hall. Negotiate a stile and a couple of steps and turn right along the track in front of the farmhouse.

4 Beyond the farmhouse, pop your dog on the lead if there are sheep in sight, and leave the track over a stile on your left. Walk along the field parallel to the lakeshore to a further stile in the far right-hand corner, ignoring a path off to the left at the end of the field. Ignore a (padlocked) fishermen's gate, instead walking to the left of and above the lakeside fence to a footpath sign. Bear left along a brief hollow way then turn right up a few steps to a kissing gate.

5 Turn left and follow the lakeside path, with mobile homes to your left. Bear right where a path straight on is blocked by barbed wire to continue around the lake. At a footpath sign, leave the Rossmere lakeside path to follow the slightly higher public footpath on the left which leads to a stile, with plenty of space for a dog to go under the fence, into a track.

6 Follow the track ahead of you (left) past houses to the crossroads with Rotherwood Road. Turn left at the crossroads, past the gates of Sylvia Cottage. Pass the Animal Sanctuary and the sign reading 'Bridle Path to Morley – No Through Road for Vehicles', and then a further sign reading 'Private No Through Road'.

❼ At a junction marked by a large stone block, turn right. Pass behind Cedar Lodge Farm until you reach the entrance to Newgate Nature Reserve; turn left onto a bridleway just beyond the reserve sign. Climb a low hill, then turn right onto a footpath joining from the right. This broad path climbs over an area of former landfill, then drops down to a junction of paths, where you carry straight on to Newgate Road.

❽ Turn left and follow the road until you reach Racecourse Road.

❾ Cross straight over, through the gate into Lindow Common, and follow the path through trees and then across open heathland to the head of Black Lake. Follow the obvious path around the far side of the lake. *Black Lake (Llyn ddu in Welsh, hence the name of the common) was originally a peaty lake fed by natural springs. It is now solely rain-fed. The lake supports various rare dragonflies, an important and thriving amphibian population, and a colony of the declining Water Vole.*

❿ Pick up a path that passes a bench and bears right, across the common between two areas of heather, shortly meeting a fence on the left. At a crossroads of paths at the end of the fence, turn left and walk out to Racecourse Road.

⓫ Cross into Lindow Lane and follow it to a T-junction beyond a house called The Nook. Turn left down a track between gardens. Carry straight on when a bridleway crosses, and follow the track past Battery House. Carry straight on when another track joins from the left.

⓬ When you meet the Rotherwood Road bridleway at a T-junction, turn left. Beyond a gate by a house, carry on along the surfaced drive and pass the end of Springfield Drive.

⓭ At the road, turn right, down Moor Lane, passing a bridleway (Clay Lane) on your left and a new housing development (The Larches) on your right.

⓮ When the metalled road bends right, take a track straight on that bends right to a gate. Follow the fenced track beyond across a field to Barlow House Farm. As you approach the farm, follow the path round to the left. At the farm entrance, turn left down the drive. When you meet the road, carry straight on to return to the Plough & Flail.

10 WOOD LANES
2¾ miles (4.3 km)

Cheshire owns a slice of the Peak District, stretching from Lyme Park in the north to the Dane valley in the south. This circular route explores the delightful country just below the high moors, bisected by the Macclesfield Canal which avoids the steepest ground. The towpath is, obviously, free of livestock, but this route also takes advantage of woodland trails and paths that pass through pastures and horse paddocks but always keep a fence or hedge between your dog and any animals.

Start & Finish: The Miners Arms, Wood Lane North, Adlington. **Sat Nav:** SK10 4PF.

How to get there: From the centre of Poynton, head towards Macclesfield on the A523 but turn left into Dickens Lane just after the Kingfisher pub. Follow the road for 1¼ miles until it meets Wood Lane West, where you turn left. After a further ½ mile turn left at a crossroads to reach the Miners Arms.

Parking: The Miners Arms has a large car park.

OS Map: Explorer 268 Wilmslow, Macclesfield & Congleton.

Grid ref: SJ937817.

THE PUB THE MINERS ARMS is right next to obvious dog-friendly routes on the Middlewood Way and Macclesfield Canal towpath so customers with dogs in tow are actively encouraged. Dogs are welcome everywhere indoors apart from in the main dining room, but in warmer weather you might prefer one of the tables out front, or to find a spot in the beer garden at the rear. Water bowls are in evidence and a jar of free doggy treats sits on the bar. ⊕ minersarmsadlington.com ☎ 01625 872731

Terrain: Canal towpath, fenced field paths and woodland trails, with a few short ascents and descents. In the wooded mid-sections of the route there are opportunities for your dog to splash about in the shallow, rocky-bedded Poynton Brook, and the canalside return allows numerous chances for a cooling drink or even a plunging swim on a hot day.

Livestock: There may be a few horses in adjacent paddocks during the first half of the walk, but the paths are safely fenced off. If your dog is prone to chasing ducks, you might want to keep him or her under close control on the canal towpath.

Stiles and roads: There are a handful of stiles, but most are easily bypassed through gaps below the rails, and one even has its own dedicated doggy gate. The only one that you might need to lift your dog over is the very first near the Miners Arms (and even here small-to medium-sized dogs will have no trouble getting under the lowest rail).

Nearest vets: Evergreen Vets, 63 London Road South, Poynton SK12 1LA. ☎ 01625 859019
Poynton Veterinary Clinic, The Veterinary Clinic, Dickens Lane, Poynton SK12 1NU. ☎ 01625 850086.

The Walk

• •

❶ From the front door of the Miners Arms, turn left past the car park entrance. Very shortly, turn left over a stile beside a field gate into a hedged track (signposted to Wardsend). At the end of the track, follow the path leading ahead between fences.

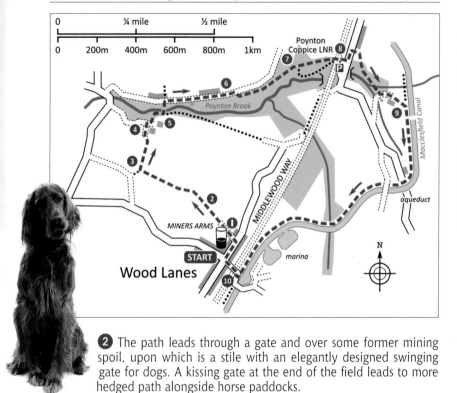

2 The path leads through a gate and over some former mining spoil, upon which is a stile with an elegantly designed swinging gate for dogs. A kissing gate at the end of the field leads to more hedged path alongside horse paddocks.

3 Ignore a path off to the left, instead following the path as it bends right to a kissing gate and beside a further paddock. A second kissing gate gives access to the end of a drive, where you walk past a house on the right.

4 Turn right at a T-junction beyond a gate, then left at the entrance to the next house onto a footpath into the woods. This path drops to meet Poynton Brook, providing an opportunity for your dog to have a drink and a splash in the flowing water.

5 Follow the brook upstream for a short distance to a footbridge, where you cross and climb some steps to a private road. You may want to slip your dog back on the lead here as the road serves several houses and you may encounter the occasional passing car though they are unlikely to be travelling at speed. Turn right, uphill slightly, passing a house on the right and then continuing to a gate by some more houses.

6 A carved post welcomes you to Poynton Coppice Local Nature Reserve. Walk a little further along the road then turn right onto a path within the wood. This path initially runs close to the road, but the latter curves away to

the left and you can let your dog off the lead as you continue through the wood past a bench to a wooden kissing gate.

7 Not long after the gate, steps on the right lead to a permissive path that loops down to the stream – over some rustic wooden bridges and stretches of boardwalk – and then climbs more steps back up again. For a less energetic walk, continue on the main footpath which winds through the trees above the valley and then drops down steps to meet the Middlewood Way. *The Middlewood Way runs for 11 miles from Marple to Macclesfield. It was opened by naturalist David Bellamy in 1985 and, in combination with the towpath of the roughly parallel Macclesfield Canal, offers lots of options for circular, dog-friendly walks, provided your dog is unfazed by the mountain bikes and horses that share the right of way.*

8 Cross the top of the car park out to the road, and turn left for a short distance. Turn into the first driveway on the right (Hideaway) and take the path to the right of the gates. This path descends into woodland via steps and over a series of bridges before climbing to a driveway. Turn left and walk past a farm before joining a footpath straight ahead, which leads up to the Macclesfield Canal. *All of its locks are concentrated into a single flight at Bosley, so there are none on this section.*

9 Turn right and follow the towpath under a footbridge (notice the remains of the mechanism of a former swing bridge on the far bank). The canal passes over an aqueduct and then under a bridge (17), continuing to a marina on the far side.

10 Just before the next bridge (18) turn right through a wooden kissing gate into a road. Turn right and follow the road over the Middlewood Way to a crossroads; turn right to return to the Miners Arms.

11 DANES MOSS & SUTTON RESERVOIR

4½ miles (7.25 km) or 3¾ miles (6 km)

This walk makes use of canal towpaths, a peatland nature reserve and an enclosed reservoir to maximise the time you can relax, secure in the knowledge that your dog will not be tempted by livestock – though intriguing smells, rustles in the undergrowth and must-have sticks may still distract them! For the humans, interest is provided by passing narrowboats, the wildlife of Danes Moss Nature Reserve, and pleasant scenery beside Sutton Reservoir and its feeder stream, with views to the hills of the Cheshire Peak District.

Only in the latter stages, after you leave the security of the reservoir, is there a strong chance of encountering cattle or sheep – either keep your dog on a tight leash if there are stock in the fields, or take the road alternative as shown on the map which will shorten your walk by ¾ mile.

Start & Finish: Sutton Hall, Bullocks Lane, Sutton. **Sat Nav:** SK11 0HE.

How to get there: If following a sat nav, make sure you have the right Sutton, Cheshire (there are more than one!). From Macclesfield, take the A523 Leek Road. Turn left into Byrons Lane (signposted to Sutton, Langley and Wincle). After ½ mile, turn right into Bullocks Lane (with a brown sign indicating Sutton Hall). Cross the canal and turn immediately left into the driveway.

Parking: Sutton Hall has a large car park for patrons; as a courtesy, please check with the bar staff before setting off on your walk.

OS Map: Explorer 268 Wilmslow, Macclesfield & Congleton.

Grid ref: SJ925715.

THE PUB **SUTTON HALL** is a Grade-II-listed building dating from the mid-1600s. Well-behaved dogs are welcome in the garden and in most of the bars. There is also a dog-watering station available outside. ⊕ brunningandprice.co.uk/suttonhall ☎ 01260 253211

THE SUTTON GAMEKEEPER, towards the end of the walk, has won awards for its food and welcomes dogs in the bar and garden. Dog biscuits and water bowls are also available. ⊕ thesuttongamekeeper.co.uk ☎ 01260 252000

Terrain: Canal towpath, level paths and boardwalks, with a few field paths and a short ascent to the dam at Sutton Reservoir. Mostly well-surfaced, but woodland and field paths may be muddy at times. Much of the route is alongside streams or the canal, so your dog is unlikely to go thirsty.
Livestock: Cattle are likely to be encountered between Sutton Reservoir and the end of the walk.
Stiles and roads: There are two stiles, both between Sutton village and Sutton Hall. There is one main road to cross and short pavement sections in Sutton village.
Nearest vets: Wright & Morten Veterinary Surgeons, 38 Cumberland Street, Macclesfield SK10 1BZ. ☎ 01625 501500.

The Walk

1 Walk out along the drive from Sutton Hall to the road. Turn right, over the canal, then drop down onto the towpath and turn right under bridge 44, the bridge you just crossed.

2 Follow the towpath for ½ mile, and pass under the A523 road (bridge 45). Continue beyond for a similar distance to bridge 46.

3 After a further ¼ mile you will reach bridge 47. *Bridge 47 is the last working swivel bridge on the canal. It was lovingly restored in 1998 by the Macclesfield Canal Society. The bridge rotates on a vertical 'king post' or pintle made of cast iron.*

CHESHIRE – Dog Friendly Pub Walks

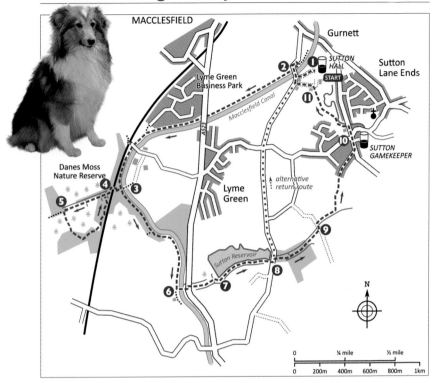

MACCLESFIELD
Gurnett
Sutton Lane Ends
SUTTON HALL
START
Lyme Green Business Park
Macclesfield Canal
A523
SUTTON GAMEKEEPER
Danes Moss Nature Reserve
Lyme Green
alternative return route
Sutton Reservoir
N

0   ¼ mile   ½ mile
0 200m 400m 600m 800m 1km

4 Turn right (away from the bridge) and cross the footbridge over the West Coast Mainline. An obvious path leads over a couple of footbridges, initially with woods on both sides, but before long you will find yourselves looking out over the open mossland on your left. *Danes Moss was formerly commercially worked for peat, as the remains of an old tramway attest. It is now under the care of the Cheshire Wildlife Trust. It is a raised bog, a rare habitat, and notable for its uncommon insects. These include the Black Darter, Britain's smallest and only black dragonfly, which can be seen on the wing from June to October. Look out also for common lizards basking on the planks of the boardwalks.*

5 Having crossed a third footbridge and passed under electricity pylons, look out for the start of a wooden boardwalk on the left. Follow this across the moss and into the trees on the far side where it bears left back toward the railway and canal. After a short open interlude below the electricity wires, the path returns to woodland and the boardwalks become intermittent, eventually leading you back to the path you used when entering the reserve. Turn right and return, over the railway footbridge, to the canal towpath, where you turn right.

6 A little after ½ mile beyond the swing-bridge, you reach bridge 48A, a more conventional footbridge. Cross the canal and turn left along the

pavement of the main road, before crossing to a kissing gate beside a gateway. Follow the path alongside the canal feeder to a footbridge at the foot of the dam. A short climb alongside an overflow channel on the right leads to a gate at the right-hand end of the dam.

7 Beyond the gate, follow the path with the reservoir on your left until you reach a road at the top end. If your dog is not comfortable around cattle, you might decide to avoid the risk of an encounter by turning left here and following the road for 1 mile back to Sutton Hall.

8 Cross the road and join a footpath more or less opposite, initially continuing along the canal feeder through trees. Put your dog on the lead as you approach a kissing gate at the end of the wood, as there may be cattle in the field beyond. Walk between two streams and continue to a gap in the fence to the right of a pretty stone bridge.

9 Cross the bridge and turn immediately right, now with the stream on your right. After a metal kissing gate, the path turns left, leaving the stream and continuing alongside a couple of fields to a gate at the end of Symondley Road. Walk down the road to the main village street, and turn left, passing the Sutton Gamekeeper on your right.

10 Pass the war memorial at a junction in the middle of the village and continue straight on, past a school entrance on your left. Before a bridge, turn left onto a streamside footpath that leads shortly to a stile. Put your dog on the lead if there are cattle in the field beyond. The path leads alongside the school grounds on your left, then swings right (with the stream again to your right) to a stile in the far corner of the field.

11 Turn left along the farm drive to the road, then right and right again into the drive to Sutton Hall.

12 ASTBURY

2¾ miles (4.5 km)

You and your dog will be among friends on this walk, as Astbury Mere is popular with dog-walkers from nearby Congleton (nicknamed Beartown). The bear is the emblem of Congleton, and the story goes that the townspeople appropriated money that had been earmarked for a new bible and spent it instead on a new bear for bear-baiting.

Most will make just a leisurely circuit of the lake, but this walk is a little more ambitious, and starts in the village of Newbold Astbury (more commonly known just as Astbury) with its fine village green, lined with pretty cottages.

Start & Finish: The Egerton Arms Country Inn, Peel Lane, Astbury. **Sat Nav:** CW12 4RQ.
How to get there: Astbury village is on the A34 Congleton to Newcastle-under-Lyme road, a mile south of Congleton (which can be reached from Junction 17 of the M6 via the A534). Leave the A34 at the Astbury turning and drive past the village green to the church; the Egerton Arms Country Inn is on the left, and the entrance to the car park is just beyond the pub.
Parking: The pub has a large car park for patrons, and there also is a small free car park by the church gateway opposite.
OS Map: Explorer 268 Wilmslow, Macclesfield & Congleton.
Grid ref: SJ845615.

THE PUB

THE EGERTON ARMS COUNTRY INN serves a range of Robinsons ales and the menu includes sandwiches and snacks as well as more substantial mains and children's meals. Dogs are most welcome in the beer garden to the rear of the pub, where there are shelters and parasols, and a dog watering station. ⊕ egertonastbury.com ☎ 01260 273946

Terrain: Field paths and surfaced lakeside paths; a little road walking. Plenty of access to Astbury Mere for water-loving dogs.

Livestock: All the fields crossed are currently under arable cultivation, so the only large animals you are likely to meet are occasional horses on the bridleways. Astbury Mere is very popular with local dog-walkers, so expect plenty of canine company.

Stiles and roads: There are no stiles; a main road is crossed twice and a short distance runs along suburban pavement.

Nearest vets: Congleton Veterinary Centre, West Heath Retail Park, Sandbach Road, Congleton, Cheshire CW12 4NB. ☎ 01260 272131.

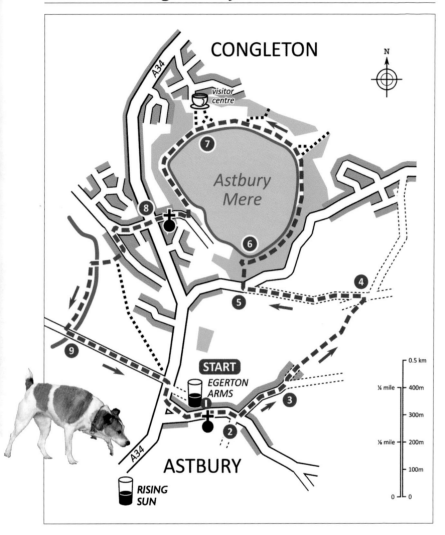

THE RISING SUN COUNTRY PUB & RESTAURANT is a 5-minute drive away in Scholar Green and allows dogs in the bar area where there are a couple of tables designated for diners with dogs. Booking ahead is advisable. Sat Nav: ST7 3JT. ⊕ risingsuncheshire.co.uk ☎ 01782 776235

The Walk

. . . .

❶ From the front door of the Egerton Arms, facing the church, turn left past the car park entrance and the village hall.

2 Turn left into School Lane, past the primary school.

3 When the road divides at a house called Potters Hill, fork left (signposted 'Congleton Town Centre') and turn right between gardens at Wits End. Beyond a kissing gate continue into an open field, which the path crosses obliquely to a further kissing gate in the hedge at the bottom. Walk along the right-hand side of the grassy field beyond the gate, then bear right between hedges and through a former kissing gate to emerge on a bridleway.

4 Turn left and follow the bridleway to the right of the gateposts for ¼ mile until you reach a road.

5 Cross over and take a path into the woodland of Astbury Mere Country Park. At the top of the hill, turn left and immediately right, picking your way down through the trees to the lakeside, to the right of the watersports centre. *Astbury Mere is owned by the Stoke-on-Trent Angling Society and maintained by*

Congleton Town Council as a country park. It occupies a former sand quarry and is 43 acres in extent. It contains good stocks of carp, perch, pike and roach, and attracts waterbirds including Great Crested Grebe, Kingfisher and Grey Heron, and occasionally rarer species such as Common Scoter and Black Tern.

6 Turn right and follow the lakeside path through the trees, ignoring any paths off to the right. Eventually you enter an open grassy area at the end of which an optional diversion leads up a path beside a bear sculpture on a pole to the Astbury Mere visitor centre and an adjacent café.

7 Suitably refreshed, return to the lakeside and resume your circuit around the lake. When you reach the road at the anglers' parking area just short of the watersports centre, slip the lead on and turn sharp right, up the road away from the lake. This bends left past new housing and a Jehovah's Witnesses Kingdom Hall to the A34.

8 Cross over into Padgbury Lane and continue past the entrance to Padgbury Close. When the road bends right, turn left. Just beyond house number 212 on the right-hand side, take a footpath between the houses. At the end of the gardens there are two kissing gates; the left is the more direct return to Astbury but the right is better used and more pleasant: turn right and cross the field to a footbridge over a stream, then turn left along the stream.

9 On reaching a metalled road (Bent Lane, which is, perversely, dead straight), turn left and follow the lane out to the A34. Cross over and either walk up the drive to the car park at the rear of the Egerton Arms or, more attractively, turn right and walk up past the cottages overlooking the village green to the church and pub.

13 RODE HEATH
4¾ miles (7.6 km)

This walk is all about salt. The outward section follows the Salt Line, a rail trail along a disused branch of the North Staffordshire Railway. A primary purpose of the railway was to deliver coal and limestone to local saltworks, and to collect salt for onward distribution to the Potteries. The return is via the Trent and Mersey Canal, here engaged in its long climb from the Cheshire Plain via the 26 locks all within 7 miles known as the Cheshire Flight (or, more colourfully, 'Heartbreak Hill': hard work for boaters, but not for walkers).

The route diverts briefly from the Salt Line on the outward leg to visit the Borrow Pit Meadows, an area of former landfill now reclaimed for conservation and recreation. Near the start is another open-access area, Rode Heath Rise, the site of a former saltworks. Both have open areas where dogs can be let off the lead under supervision.

Start & Finish: The Broughton Arms, Rode Heath. **Sat Nav:** ST7 3RU.
How to get there: The Broughton Arms is on the A533 Sandbach–Alsager road in the village of Rode Heath. From Junction 17 of the M6, follow the A534 into Sandbach and turn left (signposted 'Sandbach cemetery') at the junction with the A533. Cross the M6 overbridge and continue for a couple of miles to Rode Heath, where you will find

the Broughton Arms on your right. Alternatively, from the A500 to the north of Stoke, follow A34/A5011/A533 and the pub is on your left.
Parking: The Broughton Arms has two good-sized car parks for patrons; street parking is also available nearby.
OS Map: Explorer 268 Wilmslow, Macclesfield & Congleton.
Grid ref: SJ806571.

THE PUB **THE BROUGHTON ARMS** serves a range of cask ales from the Marston's stable. Their weekday menu includes traditional mains, but on Sundays the focus is on roast dinners. A limited selection of vegetarian dishes is available on both the everyday and Sunday menus. Dogs are welcome in the bar, and on the partially covered patio with picnic tables overlooking the canal. Water is thoughtfully provided from a 'dog bar': a converted barrel in the garden. ⊕ broughtonarmspub.co.uk ☎ 01270 883203

Terrain: Mostly level canal towpaths and rail trail; some road walking. There are occasional ponds and streams on the outward leg.
Livestock: The only animals you are likely to meet are horses and other dogs.
Stiles and roads: There are no stiles; a ¾ mile section follows a road with reasonable verges.
Nearest vets: County Vets, 9 Lawton Road, Alsager, Stoke-on-Trent ST7 2AA. ☎ 01270 882112.

The Walk

1 Cross the car park to the bridge over the canal in the rear left-hand corner. There are open spaces to right and left where you can let your dog off the lead. When you're done, take the path straight ahead, between the dog bin and the interpretation panel, which leads down steps to a bridge over a stream. Follow the path beyond to a driveway, which leads out to a road junction (dogs on leads if they're not good with traffic).

2 Turn right and follow the road for a little under ½ mile to the crossroads by the Horseshoe Inn (not dog-friendly, but there is a dog bin here).

3 Cross over and continue along Cherry Lane (a quieter no-through road) for a further ¼ mile until you meet the B5078.

4 Turn left then right onto the Salt Line (where there is another dog bin). Follow the trail, ignoring a footpath off to the left. *Look out for posts bearing the names of planets, starting with Neptune. These are part of the eye-opening Solar System Trail: the posts are placed proportionally from the 'sun' in the car park at the far end.*

5 After 700 metres, turn left through wooden barriers onto a path that runs down the side of a wood (ignore a footpath over a stile on the left). The path ahead leads to the bottom end of the pool in Borrow Pit Meadows,

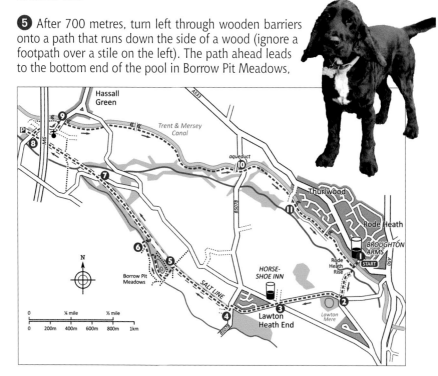

where there is a bench and a small open area for your dog to run around. Turn right onto the path that runs along the left-hand side of the lake and follow it to the top end. Turn left over a footbridge and then right along the woodland edge.

6 Bear right at a path junction by an interpretation board, and at Tilly's Bridge cross the stream again and follow the path back up to the Salt Line. Turn left.

7 After ½ mile, cross a road (where there are more dog bins) and continue along the Salt Line. Eventually, you pass under the M6 and reach the end of the trail.

8 Follow the road under the M6, and walk past the pink-painted Church of St Philip, Hassall Green.

9 At the canal bridge, drop left onto the towpath (past a dog bin) and turn right, under the bridge. Follow the canal past lock 57 and continue past a canal milepost and under bridge 146 to locks 56 and 55.

10 After ¾ mile, shortly after bridge 144, you cross an aqueduct over the B5078; continue along the towpath beyond.

11 From lock 54 onwards, the view from the towpath includes the canalside cottages of Rode Heath. Lock 53 is the last you will encounter on this route; beyond it, cross the canal at bridge 140 to return to the Broughton Arms.

14 NANTWICH & DORFOLD HALL
5¼ miles (8.3 km)

The parkland surrounds of the River Weaver and the towpath of Shropshire Union Canal provide livestock-free walking, as does an estate road through the grounds around Dorfold Hall, built in 1616. This is a walk for architecture buffs: as well as two historic churches, there are pretty cottages, a fine canal aqueduct designed by Thomas Telford and constructed in the 1820s, and you walk the length of Welsh Row, with its mixture of Tudor and Georgian houses. There are also a number of good, dog-friendly pubs passed on the route.

Start & Finish: Wilbrahams, 58 Welsh Row, Nantwich. **Sat Nav:** CW5 5EJ.

How to get there: From Junction 16 of the M6 follow the A500 and A51, then continue along the B5074 signposted to Nantwich town centre. At the Churches Mansion roundabout, go straight on into Hospital Street, then turn left at a mini-roundabout. Follow the road round to the right between Morrisons and Aldi, then go straight ahead into Water Lode at a roundabout (signposted 'Swimming pool'). Turn left when you reach Welsh Row and Wilbrahams is on the right after 200 metres.

Parking: Wilbrahams has a few car parking spaces for customers, but nearby street parking is free.
OS Map: Explorer 257 Crewe & Nantwich.
Grid ref: SJ647524.

THE PUB **WILBRAHAMS** is a bar and restaurant housed in a Grade-II-listed Georgian building. Dogs are welcome in the bar and in the outside area at the rear, and water bowls are provided.
☎ 01270 611633

Other Nantwich pubs that welcome dog-owners include **The Crown Hotel** on the High Street, **The Vine Inn** and **The Boot & Shoe** both in Hospital Street, and **The Wickstead Arms** in Mill Street. There is also a café at Nantwich Marina.

Terrain: Town-centre streets (some pedestrianised), riverside walks, level field paths and canal towpath.
Livestock: Cattle and sheep may be encountered on one short stretch between Nantwich Lake and the railway line (which is crossed at a level crossing).
Stiles and roads: There are no stiles. The walk begins in the centre of Nantwich, where shoppers and traffic can be expected.
Nearest vets: Nantwich Veterinary Hospital, Crewe Road End, CW5 5SF. ☎ 01270 610322.

The Walk

1 Walk along Welsh Row towards the town centre, and cross the River Weaver. Cross Water Lode at the pedestrian crossing and continue along High Street. Turn right into the pedestrianised area and pass the dog-friendly Crown Hotel. Bear left at the war memorial to the church.

2 Turn right in front of the church and pass through a pedestrian gate into cobbled Church Lane. Walk down to Hospital Street and turn right. At the junction with Pillory Street and High Street, turn right then immediately left

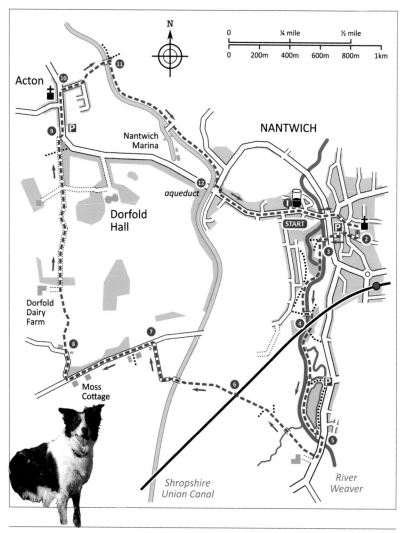

into Mill Street. Pass the dog-friendly Wickstead Arms and carry on straight down to the river.

3 Cross Water Lode at the lights and cross the bridge opposite on a path over a bridge onto Mill Island. Turn left and walk downstream for ¼ mile, following the Nantwich Riverside Loop as it crosses the millstream at a weir and keeps left by the houses of Riverside.

4 At a footbridge, cross the river (signposted Shrewbridge Road) and turn right to pass under the railway bridge. Continue along the river (now on your right) to Nantwich Lake, where you are requested to keep your dog on a lead to protect the waterfowl. Stay beside the river, with the lake on your left, to a footbridge over its outlet, beyond which you turn right and walk out to the main road.

5 Cross and turn right, over the river. Follow the road for 100 metres then, before the 'Secret Bunker' sign, cross and follow a Nantwich Riverside Loop sign into fields on the right. There are likely to be cows and sheep in the next few fields. Cross the field to a double-gated footbridge over a stream, then climb the next field, keeping right to the far corner (and ignoring a stile on the right). Beyond a sheepfold, follow the bridleway waymark through a gate ahead and follow the field boundary to a level crossing.

6 Beyond the railway, follow the fenced path to emerge on the edge of a new housing development. Continue to a canal bridge and follow the narrow Green Lane beyond it, which bends right to join Marsh Lane.

7 Put your dog on the lead and turn left along the vergeless road, passing Manor Cottages on your left. Just after the pretty Moss Cottage, turn right into Dig Lane.

8 When the lane bends left, take the farm track through the gate heading straight ahead, with a public footpath sign pointing to Acton. This leads pleasantly between hedges – you can probably take the dog off the lead – to Dorfold Dairy Farm, beyond which you cross a cattle grid and pick up a metalled estate road. Follow it for a little over ½ mile, carrying straight on at the service entrance to Dorfold Hall on the right.

9 Pass behind Grove Cottage to meet the B5341 in Acton (put the lead on if your dog isn't good around traffic). Turn left past the half-timbered former Swan Inn, now a private house, to a road junction by Acton Church.

10 Beyond the church, turn right into residential Wilbraham Road (signposted 'Crewe-Nantwich Circular Walk'). When the road bends right, take the narrow metalled path on the left, which leads past a bungalow to a gate into a field (usually arable, so you can take the lead off). Cross the field to the Shropshire Union Canal.

11 Beyond the canal, turn left down the steps, left and left again to pass under bridge 93. Follow the metalled towpath past Nantwich Marina, passing under the white-painted bridge number 92. *The Battle of Nantwich, a victory for the Parliamentarians over the Royalists, was fought in fields between the canal and river on 25 January 1644. The date is still marked in Nantwich by a celebration known as Holly Holy Day and featuring a Sealed Knot re-enactment of the battle.*

12 Continue to Nantwich Aqueduct; ignore a path off to the left for a close look at the aqueduct, then leave the canal via a flight of brick steps down the embankment. Cross Water Lode at the pedestrian crossing, then follow Welsh Row opposite, back to the town centre and the start.

15 CHURCH MINSHULL
1½ miles (2.5 km)

This short and straightforward walk is perhaps one for a day when time is limited or as part of a longer day out. It explores the pretty half-timbered village of Church Minshull and twice crosses the River Weaver. The black-and-white cottages of the village are, perhaps unusually, older than the place of worship they surround, generally dating from the 17th century. The central section of the route runs along a stretch of the Shropshire Union Canal before returning via woodland to the village.

Start & Finish: The Badger Inn, Cross Lane, Church Minshull. **Sat Nav:** CW5 6DY.
How to get there: From Over Square roundabout in Winsford (the junction of the A54 and B5074 west of the town centre), take the B5074 (signposted to Nantwich). Follow this road for 3¾ miles to the mini-roundabout in Church Minshull. Turn right past the church and the Badger Inn is immediately on your right. Alternatively, pick up the B5074 north from the Reaseheath roundabout on the A51 Nantwich bypass.
Parking: The Badger has a large car park for patrons.
OS Map: Explorer 267 Northwich & Delamere Forest.
Grid ref: SJ665605.

THE PUB

THE BADGER INN has a comfortable tap room where your dog is welcome, and behind the pub is a delightful flower-filled beer garden in the shadow of the church tower. The lunch menu includes light meals and sandwiches, which can be supplemented with a mug of hot soup. Vegetarians are well catered for and there are gluten-free choices too.

🌐 badgerinn.co.uk ☎ 01270 522348

Terrain: Canal towpath and farm tracks. Plentiful access to the River Weaver and the Shropshire Union Canal.

Livestock: Cattle may be encountered between the canal and village on the return loop, or in the small field below Old Hoolgrave Farm.

Stiles and roads: There are four stiles: larger dogs may need assistance over the two at Old Hoolgrave Farm, but the others have adjacent gates or fences with large gaps under the lowest rail.

Nearest vets: Winsford Veterinary Surgery, 84–88 High Street, Winsford, CW7 2AP. ☎ 01606 592714.
Crewe Veterinary Hospital, Macon Way, Crewe CW1 6DG.
☎ 01270 211022.

The Walk

● ●

1 From the front of the pub, cross the road and turn right then, more or less immediately, turn left into Eachus Lane. Bear right between houses then follow the lane to a farm bridge over the River Weaver.

2 Turn left over a stile immediately after the bridge and walk diagonally up to a second stile into a concrete track to the left of the farmhouse. There may be cattle in this field. Turn left and follow the track as far as a bridge over the Shropshire Union Canal.

3 Turn left down steps onto the towpath and turn left again, away from the bridge (you can safely let your dog off the lead here). Follow the canal under bridge 12 and pass a bench to

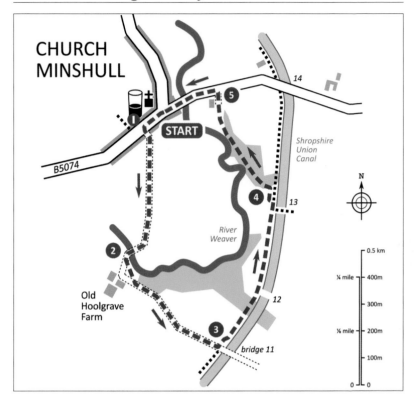

bridge 13. Shortly after bridge 13, check whether there are cattle in the field on your left, then leave the towpath via a stile on the left and bear right along the top of the field into Eardswick Wood.

4 Bear left and follow a pleasant, generally descending path through the wood, passing a bench and a couple of footbridges over boggy spots. (There's nothing to stop cows entering the wood but I saw no sign on either of my two visits.) Exit the wood at a stile and cross the field ahead, keeping close to the right-hand hedge (livestock are possible). In the far corner a stile and gate lead to a short track passing Woodside Cottage to the road.

5 Turn left and follow the busy road over the River Weaver bridge. At the mini-roundabout, go straight on past the church back to the Badger Inn. *The church that gives Church Minshull its name is neo-Classical, built in the 18th century on the site of an earlier timber-framed church.*

16 MIDDLEWICH
3½ miles (5.6 km)

This is a peaceful, leafy walk for almost its entire length, with the bonus of some interesting and historic canal and riverside architecture (well explained on interpretation boards).

When you have completed this route, you will have walked the entire length of one of Britain's historic canals. But you won't have worn out your dog's poor old pads...since the canal in question is just 150 feet long! In truth, the Wardle Canal is no more than a legal fiction, but if you count it as a separate body of water, this walk includes encounters with three different canals and three rivers.

Start & Finish: The Big Lock, Webbs Lane, Middlewich. **Sat Nav:** CW10 9DN.

How to get there: From Junction 18 of the M6, head west on the A54 (signposted to Middlewich). Carry straight on at the Salt Cellar roundabout towards the town centre. Keep right of the church on the A54 (signposted Winsford). Turn right into Pepper Street (signposted 'Middlewich Town F.C.' and 'Big Lock'). Follow the road round to the left and then right into Webbs Lane. The Big Lock pub is on the right of a bend after 350 metres.

Parking: There is a private car park for patrons at the Big Lock, and plentiful street parking nearby.
OS Map: Explorer 267 Northwich & Delamere Forest.
Grid ref: SJ702668.

THE PUB

THE BIG LOCK opens at 11.30 and serves food all day until mid-evening. Dogs are permitted in the snug and pool room (on the left as you enter) and at the canalside tables overlooking the lock. Four cask ales (Bombardier plus three guests) are on offer.
☎ 01606 738354

THE KINGS LOCK INN near point 9, on the Trent & Mersey Canal near the junction with the Wardle Canal, is also dog-friendly. ⊕ kingslockinn.com ☎ 01606 836894

Terrain: Canal towpaths, footpaths and roads. Mostly level with only moderate gradients.
Livestock: The only animals you are likely to encounter are ducks and swans on the various waterways ... and other dogs!
Stiles and roads: No stiles. A small amount of road walking and two main roads to cross.
Nearest vets: Middlewich Veterinary Surgery, 39 Newton Heath, Middlewich, CW10 9HL. ☎ 01606 833731.

The Walk

. . . .

❶ Walk either side of the Big Lock to the canal towpath at the rear, and turn left. Continue along the towpath under the bridge, with the canal on your right and a terrace of new houses on your left. Pass a reedy pond and the last of the houses, then follow the canal through open country for almost ½ mile to pass under the A530 at bridge 173.

❷ Pass a house and then a recycling centre on your left and continue along the towpath to the aqueduct over the River Dane. Here, turn left and take the right-hand of two surfaced paths, which runs parallel to the Dane on the right.

❸ After a short distance you reach the confluence of the Rivers Dane

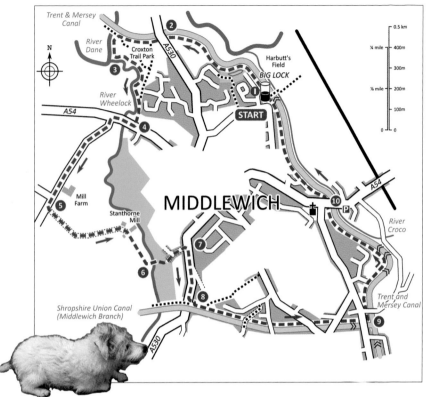

and Wheelock, and the path swings left, now following the tributary. At a path junction by a dog poo bin, turn right and follow the path out to the main road.

4 Cross and turn right along the pavement, crossing the Wheelock. Leave the main road into Coalpit Lane on the left, and follow it uphill for ¼ mile. Pass Mill Farm (on your left) and continue along the road to the junction with Birch Lane. Keep straight on.

5 Around 70 metres beyond the junction, turn left into a farm track which runs down the side of a field and then bends left to Stanthorne Mill House. Bear right in front of the mill building and pick up a narrow fenced footpath to the right of a gate beyond (a sign here requests dogs on leads). The footpath bends left and crosses the Wheelock via a bridge above a small circular weir.

6 Climb the hedged path beyond, which shortly joins a driveway. At a junction with another private drive (Mill Lane) turn right and walk out to the A530 road.

7 Turn right and walk down to the aqueduct carrying the Middlewich Branch of the Shropshire Union Canal over the main road. Cross carefully at the lights and climb brick steps up to the canal towpath above.

8 Turn left and follow the towpath for ½ mile to Wardle Lock, passing under four intervening bridges (numbered 28 to 31). Beyond Wardle Lock follow the towpath under a fifth bridge (Wardle Bridge, 168) to the junction with the Trent & Mersey Canal.

9 Turn left along the new towpath and pass under white-painted bridge number 169, through a metal barrier and under a canopied building. Continue past locks 72, 73 and 74 in quick succession, and pass another canopied shelter. At Town Bridge there is an opportunity to turn left, away from the canal, and visit the town centre.

10 Otherwise, pass under Town Bridge and continue along the towpath for a further 700 metres back to the Big Lock.

17 PETTY POOL & WHITEGATE

5½ miles (8.9 km)

A permissive path allows through access to Petty Pool, a pretty and secluded wooded lake that is probably unknown even to some locals. Much of the surrounding area belonged to Vale Royal Abbey, an important Cistercian hub founded by Edward I. He originally had great ambitions for the foundation, but his interest wandered and it was eventually closed by Henry VIII during the Dissolution of the Monasteries, and is now a private golf club.

As well as the lakes, and pretty Whitegate village, this walk includes attractive woodland and an easy, traffic-free section of the Whitegate Way, a former railway line.

Start & Finish: The Plough Inn, Beauty Bank, Whitegate. **Sat Nav:** CW8 2BP.
How to get there: The Plough is hidden away on a rural cul-de-sac. From the Salterswall Roundabout on the A54 west of Winsford, follow the B5074 signposted to Whitegate and Vale Royal Abbey. Turn left at

the next junction and follow Whitegate Road for ½ mile, before passing under the former railway line of the Whitegate Way. Keep right at the next junction, then turn right at a crossroads, into a no-through road (Beauty Bank), indicated by a sign for the Plough.

Parking: The Plough has a reasonably large car park, for patrons only. Please check with staff before leaving your car. There are alternative car parks on the route (see map).

OS Map: Explorer 267 Northwich & Delamere Forest.

Grid ref: SJ623682.

THE PUB

THE PLOUGH INN, while locally renowned as a dining destination, welcomes dog-walkers too, with prominent blackboards indicating that well-behaved dogs are welcome in the tap room. Alternatively, the flower-hung frontage and parasols shelter picnic tables where you and your dog can rest after your walk on a fine day. ⊕ ploughwhitegate.com ☎ 01606 889455

Terrain: Lakeside woodlands and farmland, village and rail trail. Dogs are explicitly excluded from the surrounds of the fishing lake at New Pool, but will appreciate the opportunity of a drink from the streams in the adjacent wood.

Livestock: There are a couple of very short stretches where you may encounter livestock, most probably cattle (noted in the text). Horse-riders and cyclists may be encountered on the Whitegate Way.

Stiles and roads: There are a handful of stiles, most easily bypassed or next to fences where all but the biggest dogs should be able to pass under the lowest wire. For ½ mile into Whitegate village, the route follows a road (with pavement).

Nearest vets: Hollybank Veterinary Centre, 584 Chester Road, Sandiway, CW8 2DX. ☎ 01606 880890.

CHESHIRE – Dog Friendly Pub Walks

There is also a dog-friendly café, with toilets and picnic area, at the former Whitegate Station during the latter stages of the walk. ⊕ whitegatestation.org.uk ☎ 01606 889567

The Walk

. . . .

❶ From the front door of The Plough, turn right along the road. When the road bears left, take the shaded path ahead, which leads shortly to another road (dogs on leads).

❷ Turn right along the pavement past the 40mph signs, then almost immediately right again through a kissing gate. The fenced path leads alongside a paddock before descending and then climbing to meet a narrow lane. Take the stony byway opposite until you meet another road.

❸ Cross and turn right down the pavement, passing

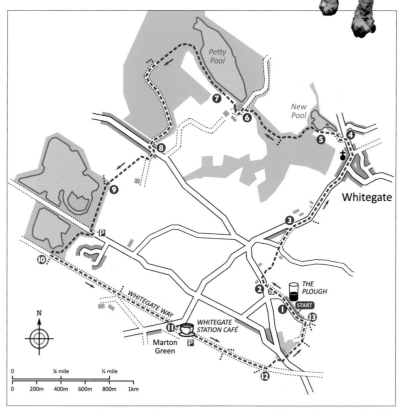

Bawsgate Farm on the left and descending to Whitegate village. Continue straight on past the primary school, and walk through the churchyard, exiting via the lychgate, and turn left opposite the Vale Royal Abbey Lodge.

4 After a short vergeless stretch, turn left into a fishermen's car park. The official line leads through the field on the right between two kissing gates, but you can avoid any potential meeting with livestock by following the track through the gateway to a second parking area.

5 Go through a gate and follow the path with a lake to your right (the lake is private, with dogs expressly forbidden). The path bends left into trees and continues via a series of bridges and boardwalks, alongside and between marshy streams.

6 At the end of a long boardwalk, a footbridge over a stream leads to a gate into a field (check for cattle and slip your dog onto the lead if necessary). Turn right to a stile into a farm track. Turn left along a permissive path past the tiny thatched Keeper's Cottage. Bear right and climb towards Pettypool Farm, before turning right through a gate into a narrow path running outside a garden fence. At the end of this stretch, a barrier leads into a field where again there may be cattle or other livestock; walk down with the lake on your right to a stile into woodland, where you can let the dog off the lead.

7 A wooded path leads parallel to the lakeside before curving left away from the open water, with a stream valley on your right. At a Peak and Northern

CHESHIRE – Dog Friendly Pub Walks

Footpath Society sign, ignore the path to Daleford and Sandiway on the right and continue along the main track signposted to Newchurch Common, which climbs more steeply through the trees before bearing right past some paddocks on the left to a metal barrier and out to the road.

8 Cross and take a few steps to the left before turning right into the driveway to Lapwing Hall Farm. Beyond the first house on the right, turn right over a stile into a narrow path between hedge and fence to a second stile. Bear left through more open grassland with patches of heather to a gate, then bear half-right across an arable field to a similar gate in the far corner.

9 On entering a belt of trees, join a sandy track at a waymark post, and follow it as it winds through conifers to a small parking area, beyond which a gate leads into a stony track. Turn left and look out for a path on the right which doubles back with a fence on the left, then bends left at the field corner. Follow this path along the fence, with glimpses to a large sand pit on your right, then bend right and left to meet the Whitegate Way. *The Whitegate Way follows a former branch line of the Mid-Cheshire Railway. Although principally built for freight, particularly salt from the Winsford works, limited passenger services ran intermittently along the line from its opening in 1870 until they were finally withdrawn in 1931.*

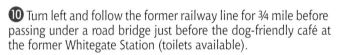
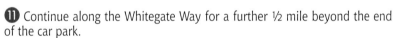

10 Turn left and follow the former railway line for ¾ mile before passing under a road bridge just before the dog-friendly café at the former Whitegate Station (toilets available).

11 Continue along the Whitegate Way for a further ½ mile beyond the end of the car park.

12 Shortly after a picnic table on the left, turn left onto a descending path which bends right on its way out to a road. Cross the stile opposite and beyond a brackeny area follow the left-hand side of the field uphill to a further stile beside a field gate.

13 Turn right along the driveway out to the road, then turn left to return to the Plough Inn.

18 DELAMERE FOREST & EDDISBURY HILLFORT

4 miles (6.4 km)

Delamere Forest is the largest and most accessible area of woodland in Cheshire, but this obvious appeal comes at a cost: the area around Blakemere and the Linmere Lodge Visitor Centre is often overwhelmingly busy with visitors. This walk avoids the crowds by exploring a quieter, more peripheral part of the Forest (at the expense of some road walking at the beginning and end). It also includes two airy hilltops with superb views over seven counties.

> **Start & Finish:** Vale Royal Abbey Arms, Chester Road, Oakmere. **Sat Nav:** CW8 2HB.
> **How to get there:** The walk starts from the junction of the A556 and B5152 between Northwich and Chester. For the pub car park, turn off the A556 onto the B5152 (signposted towards Tarporley) and turn immediately left.

Parking: The pub has a large car park for patrons, or there is a layby on the A556 just west of the entrance to St Peter's Church (see map).
OS Map: Explorer 267 Northwich & Delamere Forest.
Grid ref: SJ563686.

THE PUB **VALE ROYAL ABBEY ARMS** is open all day, from 11am during the week (food served from noon) and from 10am (for breakfast) at weekends. Dogs are welcome in the bar and conservatory and on the terrace at the rear of the building. Dog biscuits are available – in return for a charitable donation – from the bar, and there is a beer-barrel water dispenser by the door from the car park. Beers, including cask ales and craft lagers, are from the J. W. Lees brewery and its offshoots.
⊕ valeroyalabbeyarms.co.uk ☎ 01606 882747

Terrain: Permissive paths and footpaths in Delamere Forest. Some road walking.
Livestock: Some fields may contain cattle, particularly in summer, but these can be bypassed as noted in the route description.
Stiles and roads: There are no stiles. The opening section is along the pavement of the busy A556; expect fast-moving traffic.
Nearest vets: Hollybank Veterinary Centre, 584 Chester Road, Sandiway, CW8 2DX. ☎ 01606 880890 or The Firs Veterinary Surgery, 4 Church St, Kelsall, CW6 0QG. ☎ 01829 751500.

The Walk

① From the car park of the Vale Royal Abbey Arms, cross the A556 at the traffic island near the bus stop, then turn left along the verge beside the busy road. Cross the B5152 (signposted to Frodsham, Kingsley and Delamere Forest) and continue along the pavement beside the A556.

② After 400 metres, you may wish to turn right for a respite from the traffic and to view St Peter's Church, built in 1817. *It is said to be a 'Waterloo church', built to celebrate and give thanks for Wellington's victory two years earlier.*

③ Returning to the main road, continue west for a further 750 metres until you reach the end of Stoney Lane by the Gothic building of Delamere C of E primary school. Turn right and walk up Stoney Lane past some houses on the left and cross the entrance to Watling Drive.

④ When Stoney Lane bends to the right at Old Pale Cottages, turn left through a kissing gate onto a footpath running along the top of an arable field.

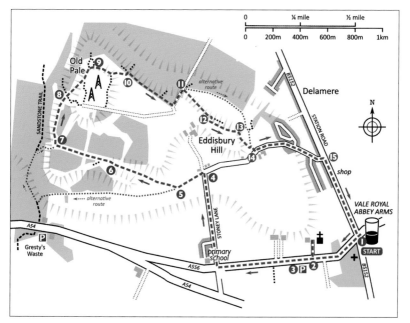

5 At a gate, check for cattle in the grassy side valley to your right. If there are none present, or your dog is used to cows, turn right through the wooden kissing gate and follow the fence before continuing up the valley below a sandstone outcrop on your right. If livestock are present and you wish to avoid them, you can continue ahead to the Sandstone Trail, turning right and then right again to regain the described route at step 7 (see map). *This rocky valley, like the slightly better-known and narrower Urchin's Kitchen in the woods south of the A54, is an Ice-Age drainage channel, excavated by meltwater running under pressure beneath an ice sheet.*

6 At the top of the valley, go through a wooden hand gate next to the field gate and bear slightly right onto a grassy track ahead (dogs can safely be let off the lead). Cross a transverse ride and continue until you meet a stony path, where you turn right.

7 Pass through the hedge and follow the path up the slope to a white Sandstone Way marker. Continue along a shelf overlooking Delamere Forest and the Mersey Estuary, passing a bench on the right.

8 Cross a track and continue ahead on the path running below a covered reservoir, which climbs to a bench then runs along the brow of the hill to the Old Pale topograph (cows in adjacent fields).

9 Take a track to the right (between the stones for Derbyshire and Staffordshire) and follow it downhill, with the masts still on your right. Ignore a path heading off to the right. When you reach the woodland edge, go through the gap in the hedge then turn immediately right, with the wood on your left and the hedge on your right.

10 Follow the woodland edge until you reach a metalled farm track. Turn left. Walk downhill for 200 metres, then turn right off the road, through a gate.

11 A visit to Eddisbury hillfort is recommended, but you are likely to find cattle grazing on the ramparts. If you prefer to forgo the hillfort and avoid any potential bovine encounter, take the path on the left that runs along the top of the woodland, then turn right to rejoin the described route at point 14 (see map); otherwise turn immediately right (before the bench) and follow the right-hand edge of the field, towards the visible embankment at the top of the slope.

12 At the top of the hill, just before the track passes between two facing metal gates, squeeze between three stakes on the right and climb to the obvious earthwork of Eddisbury hillfort. *Eddisbury is the largest and most complex* *of Cheshire's hillforts. It was built in the Iron Age, deliberately slighted by the Romans, then re-occupied during the Dark Ages. The northern ramparts survive reasonably well, and the eastern entrance was reconstructed following an excavation in 2010.*

13 Follow the rampart until you reach the reconstructed entrance; here, drop down between low rock outcrops towards a lower path. At an interpretation panel set in a large rock, negotiate the stile and emerge into the quiet road.

14 Turn left and walk past Eddisbury Hill Farm, then through a caravan park.

15 On meeting Station Road at the bottom of the hill, turn right and follow the pavement past Delamere Stores and the community centre back to the A556 and the Vale Royal Abbey Arms.

19 PECKFORTON HILLS
3¼ miles (5 km)

The Pheasant is one of Cheshire's destination pubs. Those that make it through the warren of country lanes will be rewarded with a warm welcome and superb views westwards over the Dee valley towards the Welsh hills. The elevation is provided by the pub's position on the mid-Cheshire ridge, here part of the Peckforton Estate. The two castles of Peckforton (Victorian imitation) and Beeston (genuine medieval) are an obvious attraction, and a visit to Beeston Castle, which is in the care of English Heritage, is an obvious extension to your day out (entrance fee; dogs on leads permitted).

Start & Finish: The Pheasant Inn, Higher Burwardsley, Tattenhall.
Sat Nav: CH3 9PF.
How to get there: The Pheasant Inn is hidden away under the wooded mid-Cheshire ridge amid a maze of country lanes, and finding the place is all part of the adventure (beware sat navs that may direct you along inaccessible byways). The simplest approach is to follow signs for 'Candle Workshops' from the A534 (between Farndon and Nantwich) or from the A49 (between Tarporley and Bunbury) via Harthill or Beeston respectively. The pub is signposted from Burwardsley Village Store.

Parking: The Pheasant has a sizeable car park for patrons, but at busy times check with the bar staff before leaving your car.
OS Map: Explorer 257 Crewe & Nantwich.
Grid ref: SJ523565.

THE PHEASANT INN is a hidden gem; the terrace outside is a marvellous place to watch the sun go down over the Welsh hills and there is a secluded garden alongside the pub. Dogs are welcome throughout (including in the rooms) and water bowls are provided.
⊕ thepheasantinn.co.uk ☎ 01829 770434

Terrain: Mostly woodland paths, some road walking and an (optional) section through pastureland. Two noticeable climbs and occasional rough ground. Woodland paths may be muddy in winter. The Peckforton Estate insists that dogs be kept on leads within their woodlands.
Livestock: Cattle may be encountered on the (avoidable) slopes above Peckforton.
Stiles and roads: There are several stiles, though all but the largest dogs should be able to bypass them. The central section of the route is along a fairly quiet lane, with adequate verges. Off-road vehicles may occasionally be encountered on a couple of the woodland drives.
Nearest vets: Birch Heath Veterinary Clinic, Birch Heath Road, Tarporley, CW6 9UU. ☎ 01829 733777.

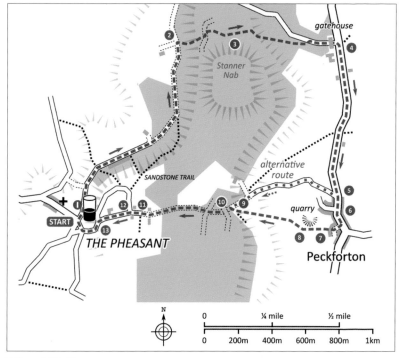

The Walk

1 From the front of the pub, turn right and follow the no-through lane past Pennsylvania Cottage and below the car park. Ignore a couple of footpaths to left and right and continue past further cottages to a gate into the Peckforton Estate (dogs on leads). Climb between sunken banks until the Sandstone Trail joins from the right. Follow the track beyond to a crossing path above a dwelling. *The Sandstone Trail runs for 34 miles from Frodsham to Whitchurch in Shropshire, mostly following the mid-Cheshire ridge, of which the Peckforton Hills are a prominent part.*

2 Turn right onto a path that winds through the trees, before climbing steeply over wooden steps to meet an estate road below a gate. Turn left, then shortly right at a waymark before another gate, with the steep slope of Stanner Nab to your right.

3 Follow the path as it descends through the woods until it meets the approach road for Peckforton Castle. Turn right and walk past an automatic vehicular barrier and through the gatehouse and out to the public road (no

pavement). *The sandstone gatehouse, built in the 1840s, is contemporary with Peckforton Castle and designed by the same architect, Anthony Salvin. The motto 'Confido Conquiesco' ('I trust and am content') is the motto of the Tollemache family. Peckforton Castle, now a hotel and wedding venue, was built for the 1st Baron Tollemache, the largest landowner in Cheshire at the time.*

4 Turn right and follow the road for ½ mile to Peckforton village. If you wish to avoid any chance of an encounter with cattle, turn right into Hill Road and follow it (and the cobbled byway it develops into) to rejoin the described route at point 9.

5 If you are confident that your dog will be unfazed by a potential bovine encounter, continue along the road through the village below the hill.

6 Continue for a further 100 metres, then turn right past the aptly named Black and White Cottage. As the driveway swings left to another house, take the footpath on the right which leads between back gardens and conifers to a shallow ladder stile (easily bypassed by dogs). If there are cattle in the fields beyond, slip your dog onto the lead.

7 Pass an old, gnarled oak tree on your right and continue up the grassy slope; a deep disused sandstone quarry lurks behind the fence on your right.

8 At the top of the quarry, pass a step stile and follow the path ahead to a fingerpost by another stile. Follow the fence on your left as the gradient increases, then at the fence corner, strike out up the hill to the right of a couple of oak trees.

9 In the top right-hand corner of the field, a final stile leads into a shady byway. Turn left.

10 Pass under a stone archway and follow the track beyond through brackeny woodland. Ignore a crossing track, occasionally used by off-road vehicles.

11 After a gate, the track leads past a house on the right and the Sandstone Trail briefly joins through a kissing gate on your left; continue along the lane, now metalled.

12 At a junction between pretty stone cottages, the Sandstone Trail turns right but our route continues straight ahead, shortly passing Rockhouse Farm on the right.

13 At another road junction, keep left and continue to the crossroads at the bottom of Rock Lane. Turn right to return to the Pheasant Inn.

20 FARNDON & HOLT

2 miles (3 km)

There can't be many walks that pack so much interest into two miles: you will encounter two medieval churches with Civil War associations, the remains of a historic castle, an ancient bridge, a boardwalk path below a geologically important cliff, and a major river.

Holt Castle, beside the River Dee, is surrounded by an extensive, safely enclosed grassy area that is great for letting the dog off the lead for a run around. What's more, there are two dog-friendly pubs, and a couple of places where you can get a coffee (with outside tables) if that's your preference.

Start & Finish: The Farndon, High Street, Farndon. **Sat Nav:** CH3 6PU.

How to get there: Farndon is bypassed by the A534 between Nantwich and Wrexham. From the east, turn right off the A534 onto the B5130 (signposted to Chester and Farndon) and then turn left. Follow the road for ½ mile into the village to find the pub on your left. From the west, take the B5102 (signposted to Holt and Rossett); follow it through the village of Holt (keeping right at the White Lion) and cross the Dee bridge, and the pub is on your right partway up the hill.

Parking: The Farndon has a car park for patrons, and there is ample street parking nearby. Alternatively, there is a signposted free car park behind the village hall (near the church).
OS Map: Explorer 257 Crewe & Nantwich.
Grid ref: SJ412545.

THE PUB

THE FARNDON is open from 5pm during the week, from 2pm on Saturday and from noon on Sundays. Dogs are welcome on the ground floor and in the gardens, and treats and water bowls are provided. Dog-friendly accommodation is available if booked in advance.
⊕ thefarndonpubfarndon.co.uk
☎ 01829 270376

THE PEAL O' BELLS in Holt is open from 4pm Monday to Friday and from noon the rest of the week (serving food till 8pm, or 5pm on Sundays) and also offers dog treats and water bowls. There is a pleasant garden overlooking the church to the rear, with play equipment for children.
⊕ pealobellsholt.co.uk ☎ 01829 270411

There are also cafés in Farndon (**Lewis's**) and Holt (**Cleopatra's**) with outside tables for dog-owners.

Terrain: Riverside paths and village streets. Several flights of steps.
Livestock: Riverside fields on the return journey may occasionally contain livestock.
Stiles and roads: Three staircases but no stiles. Some roadside walking, including the Dee crossing alongside fast-moving traffic on the A534. Water: plentiful, as much of the walk is alongside the River Dee.
Nearest vets: Gatehouse Veterinary Centre; branches at Chester Road, Lavister, Rossett, LL12 0DF.
☎ 01244 570364, or 2 Borras Park Road, Borras, Wrexham, LL12 7TG. ☎ 01978 310131.

The Walk

. . . .

1 Turn left down the main village street to the bridge and cross the River Dee into Wales. *Farndon Bridge was built in 1339. It originally had a gatehouse and drawbridge on the fifth arch.*

2 Continue up the hill into Holt. You may wish to divert left, either into the Peal o' Bells pub or to visit the church of St Chad. *St Chad's has much of interest, including a leaning pillar, a nicely carved heraldic 15th-century font, and obvious bullet holes in the wall, the result of hand-to-hand combat inside the church during the Civil War.*

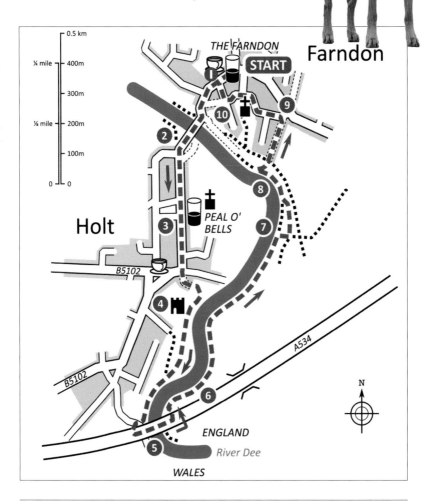

3 Continue along the main street, passing the entrance to Vicarage Court, until it bends to the right, where you leave it to cross Deeside and continue into Castle Garden (signposted to the Castle). Bear left past the former school then take a footpath on the left which leads downhill through trees and then bends right to emerge beside the river near the Castle where you can safely let your dog off the lead. *Holt Castle was begun by Edward I after the invasion of North Wales in 1277. The impressive five-towered castle was complete by 1311, but the castle was already greatly diminished by the 1500s and much of the remaining stonework was taken away by Sir Thomas Grosvenor to build Eaton Hall, a few miles down the Dee.*

4 Pass the castle ruin with the river on your left, and walk below a dragonfly sculpture. You pass some red sandstone cliffs on your right and go through a wooden kissing gate into a lane. You may want to slip your dog on the lead at this point, as you will encounter traffic, and possibly cattle, shortly. Bear right for a short distance, then turn left onto a path that leads to a metal kissing gate to some metal steps up to the main road.

5 Turn left and cross the River Dee. Immediately beyond the end of the bridge parapet on the English side, step over the crash barrier on your left and walk down the steps to the riverbank. Turn right, checking for livestock in the field ahead.

6 Follow the riverside path through two fields separated by a metal kissing gate, with views back over the river to Holt Castle. After a second kissing gate, continue through a weedy area to a wire-fenced bridge where a ditch meets the river.

7 Beyond this, turn right, away from the river. At a path junction bear left, then turn left again onto a boardwalk which winds below sandstone cliffs for 150 metres back to the riverside path.

8 Continue along a concrete path with a handrail through woods. At the end of the concrete path, turn right on a path that leads to a flight of steps with the cliff-face on the right. Turn right and left into Old Lane (a driveway) and walk out to its junction with Church Lane.

9 Turn left, and then go through the gates into the churchyard. Walk past the church and exit via another gate on the far side.

10 Walk down Church Lane to a junction, where you turn right (ignoring the bollarded-off lane straight ahead). Church Lane emerges opposite the Greyhound pub (closed at the time of writing), where you turn right to return to the Farndon.

A SELECTION OF OTHER DOG FRIENDLY COUNTRY PUBS IN CHESHIRE

ACTON BRIDGE – Hazel Pear
ALPRAHAM – Tollemache Arms
ANDERTON – Stanley Arms
ANTROBUS – Antrobus Arms
ASTBURY – Horse Shoe
BARTHOMLEY – White Lion
BOLLINGTON – Dog & Partridge
BOSLEY – Harrington Arms
BOSTOCK GREEN – Hayhurst Arms
BRERETON GREEN – Bear's Head
BUGLAWTON – Church House
BULKELEY – Bickerton Poacher
BUNBURY – Dysart Arms
CHRISTLETON – Ring o' Bells
COMBERBACH – Spinner & Bergamot
COMPSTALL – Andrew Arms
COTEBROOK – Fox and Barrel
DARESBURY – Ring o' Bells
DELAMERE – Carriers Inn, Fishpool Inn
DISLEY – Dandy Cock

DUNHAM–ON–THE–HILL – Wheatsheaf
EATON – Waggon & Horses
GAWSWORTH – Harrington Arms
GRAPPENHALL – Parr Arms
GREAT BUDWORTH – Cock O'Budworth, George and Dragon
HALE – Childe of Hale
HALE BARNS – Bulls Head
HAPSFORD – Hornsmill at Helsby
HASLINGTON – Hawk Inn
HAUGHTON MOSS – Nag's Head
HENBURY – Cock
HURDSFIELD – Three Crowns
KELSALL – Farmers Arms
LITTLE BUDWORTH – Egerton Arms, Red Lion, Shrewsbury Arms
LITTLE LEIGH – Leigh Arms
LOWER WHITLEY – Chetwode Arms
LYMM – Crown, Jolly Thresher
MARPLE – Bulls Head, Navigation
MARSTON – Salt Barge
MATLEY – Rising Moon
MELLOR – Devonshire Arms
MILL BROW – Hare & Hounds
MOBBERLEY – Church Inn
OLLERTON – Dun Cow
PLUMLEY – Golden Pheasant, Smoker
POYNTON – Cask Tavern
PRESTBURY – Ye Olde Admiral Rodney
SANDBACH – Old Hall
SPURSTOW – Yew Tree
STOAK – Bunbury Arms
TARPORLEY – Rising Sun
TATTENHALL – Letters Inn
TIVERTON – Shady Oak
WARMINGHAM – Bear's Paw
WHITELEY GREEN – Windmill
WRENBURY – Dusty Miller